The FLAVOURS *of* NATIONALISM

A Memoir

with Recipes *for* Love, Hate *and* Friendship

NANDITA HAKSAR

SPEAKING TIGER

SPEAKING TIGER BOOKS LLP
125A, Ground Floor,
Shahpur Jat, New Delhi 110049

First published in paperback by Speaking Tiger 2018
This revised edition published in 2022

All photos inside the book are courtesy the author, except photos on page v (by Biswajit Ganguly), page 16 (by David Lisbona), page 87 (by Sahil Tiwari) and page 213 (by Saad Akhtar), all of which are courtesy Wikimedia Commons.

10 9 8 7 6 5 4 3 2 1

ISBN: 978-93-5447-113-1
e-ISBN: 978-93-5447-121-6

Typeset in Adobe Garamond Pro at SÜRYA, New Delhi
Printed at Gopsons Papers Ltd.

To the street vendors,
in solidarity with their struggles

CONTENTS

BY WAY OF AN INTRODUCTION

THE JUSTICE OF EATING

Hunger feels like pincers,
like the bite of crabs,
it burns and has no fire.
Hunger is a cold fire.
Let us sit down to eat
with all those who haven't eaten;
let us spread great tablecloths,
put salt in the lakes of the world,
set up planetary bakeries,
tables with strawberries in snow,
and a plate like the moon itself
from which we can all eat.
For now I ask no more
than the justice of eating.

— Pablo Neruda, 'The Great Tablecloth'
(translated by Alastair Reid)

When I wrote *Flavours of Nationalism*, it did not even remotely occur to me that the book would get such a warm reception. A year after its publication in 2018, it was chosen for the Gourmand World Awards in two categories, 'Cookbook for Peace' and 'Food Writing'. I was so surprised that I wrote to the Gourmands to ask whether the report was accurate. To my greater surprise, the Living Foodz Epicurean Guild of India chose it as their book of the year, and I found myself among celebrity chefs and food writers in a five-star hotel waiting to receive the award. I asked the organizers what had made them pick this book, because it is not really a cookbook or even a very scholarly work based on original research. I was told that *Flavours* was chosen for 'asking that uncomfortable question: How can a people who won't eat together, stay united?'

And indeed, in the course of writing this book I had realized that we were perhaps the only country in the world where there had been serious debates even among our freedom fighters about whether it was right and proper to eat with fellow country people who belonged to different castes or religious communities.

But I hadn't started off with this thought.

~

The idea of writing a book on the different cuisines in India came to me when I attended my first human-rights conference in the early 1980s, in Amritsar. I had just begun my life as a human-rights lawyer; it was a new and exciting world for me. I met people from all over India and made friends, heard inspiring speeches and got to know people who had dedicated their lives to fighting state repression. Many had risked their lives, jobs and security for justice. The food at the conference was fabulous. I loved the dal makhani, and the rotis from the tandoor were soft, unlike the ones we got in Delhi. We had almost finished the lunch when I heard a comrade from Andhra, a member of the Organization for Civil and Democratic Rights (OCDR), ask one of the local comrades: 'Is there any rasam?'

Having been brought up with the Nehruvian idea that we must appreciate the cultures and cuisines of others, I was outraged with the man for not appreciating the Punjabi food on offer. Doing so was the essence of the unity in diversity ideal.

And then I saw the humour in the situation and laughed to myself. That was when I thought I would write a book called 'Rasam in Amritsar'. So, in a sense, this book was born some forty years ago.

When I got married to a fellow student at Jawaharlal Nehru University (JNU), almost everyone, even human-rights activists, would smile and ask, 'Does he eat dogs?' This was meant to be humour. My husband Sebastian is from the Tangkhul Naga tribe in Manipur. I never knew how to respond; should I shock them by saying yes, he ate dog meat, or tell them the truth, that he did not eat dog meat because he was allergic to it? Most days I would answer: 'No, Sebastian does not eat dog meat. But I do.' I dealt with variations of this question, brazenly asked or hinted, for years. It still comes up.

All this while, the idea of the book stayed with me. I wanted to write something light-hearted; something to make us laugh at ourselves and our everyday prejudices. But as the book progressed, it became grim.

~

The warm response to the first edition of *Flavours* encouraged me to think of other aspects of nationalism, and I finally decided on three further memoirs, making a quartet, each volume independent of the others but all four linked by my endeavour to grapple with various aspects of Indian nationalism. The next volume in the series will be *The Colours of Nationalism*, to be followed by *The Deceptions of Nationalism* and finally by an as yet untitled book about Indian nationalism abroad, specifically, eastern Africa.

There is rich debate on the virtues of patriotism and dangers of nationalism. Some philosophers have warned us about patriotism, too; about how it can lead to distortions of ethics and judgement.* This book is not really a part of those conversations, but it engages with the larger idea behind them.

I am a patriot, and would even describe myself as an Indian nationalist. I have all my life been obsessed with the idea of India. The metaphor for India has so often been a garden with flowers of myriad colours, and birds of different shapes and sizes singing their many songs under one blue sky. But now, everything—even food—has been divided along religious lines. I grew up singing 'Saare Jahan se achha, Hindustan hamaara / Hum bulbulein hain isski, yeh gulsitaan hamara' (Our Hindustan is better than all the world / We are its songbirds, it is our garden), but today's generation laments, 'Nafraton ka asar dekho' (Look, This is the Consequence of Hate):

> Such are the effects of hate, even animals have been divided,
> The cow has become Hindu, the goat is now a Muslim.
>
> The trees, the leaves and branches are troubled,
> For birds too may become Hindu and Muslim.
>
> The dry fruits are all very confused,
> Should coconuts now be Hindu and dates Muslim?
>
> The way religion is dividing everything—
> That green is the colour of Muslims and red the colour of
> Hindus—
> The day isn't far when every green vegetable will belong to
> Muslims
> And Hindus will be left with just carrots and tomatoes.

*For a philosophical debate of patriotism see John Kleining, Simon Keller and Igor Primoratz, *The Ethics of Patriotism: A Debate*, John Willey and Sons, 2015.

Now here is a conundrum:
Where does the poor watermelon belong?
Will it be Muslim on the outside and Hindu inside?

This poem, originally in Urdu, has gone viral on the internet. It was written in 2015 by Javed Jaffrey, the famous Bollywood actor and comedian. He is the son of Syed Ishtiaq Ahmed Jaffrey (1939-2020) who, like many Muslim actors, went by a Hindu name: Jagdeep.

~

This book was written in the background of the controversies raging in India over beef-eating and the meaning of vegetarianism in our culture and society. After the BJP came to power at the Centre in May 2014, even academic discussion on the subject was forbidden, and Muslim and Dalit citizens of India began to be lynched, with complete impunity, on suspicion of eating beef, for transporting cattle, or for no reason at all. A documentary film called *Caste on the Menu Card* made by students of the prestigious Tata Institute of Social Sciences was banned from the Jeevika Film Festival by the Ministry of Information and Broadcasting, and permission was denied for an alternative screening at JNU.

The issue is not only about a religious taboo but the hypocrisy of such a ban, which is brought out in this poem written in Telugu by a Dalit poet, Digumarthi Suresh Kumar:

When you drove me far from the village,
When you found even my footprints untouchable,
When you couldn't even see me as human,
What stood by me
And brought me here was beef.
[…]

When its udders were squeezed and milked
You didn't feel any pain at all,
When it was stitched into a chappal you stamped...and
walked on
You didn't feel any hurt,
When it rang as a drum at your marriage and your funeral
You didn't suffer any blows;
When it sated my hunger, beef became your goddess?*

Of course, it is not only Dalits and Muslims who eat beef; most of the people in the eight states of India's Northeast and in other parts of the country such as Goa and Kerala also eat beef, as they have done for millennia. Historians and ancient literature tell us the so-called Vedic people also ate beef. Those who impose beef bans and encourage, even engineer, mob lynchings and targeted killings, know this only too well. They also know that even the ordinary Hindus who do not eat beef themselves will live amicably with those who do. I saw evidence of this everywhere, including a semi-urban village on the outskirts of Delhi, which incident I have recorded in this book—a traditional Hindu family and an Afghan Muslim refugee living in harmony, with mutual respect and affection. That is the kind of humanity and nationalism I value; the kind of nationalism that can bring us back from the precipice that communal hate and majoritarian politics have dragged us to.

~

Since the book was first published, two major events have taken place which have also had a direct bearing on the issues that I tried to raise in it.

*Translation by Naren Bedide.

The first was the national lockdown imposed at just four hours' notice in March 2020 to control the spread of the coronavirus. And the second was the introduction of new farm laws by the central government which brought protesting farmers to the borders of Delhi, the seat of absolute power.

Overnight, on 23 March 2020, the 53,000 hotels and 70 lakh restaurants of India's organized sector and 2.3 crore eateries in the unorganized sector were closed down and several lakh employees of these establishments—among crores of other workers—became jobless. Most of these people were migrant workers. The images of hundreds of thousands of migrant workers walking back from the cities to their homes in villages hundreds of kilometers away, with little to eat and at the mercy of the elements, still haunt me.

The tragedy of each individual life among our vulnerable—and now abandoned—fellow citizens was made deeper by the callousness of many of our celebrities who, in the middle of all this, were busy posting pictures on their twitter and instagram accounts of the cakes and gluten-free breads they were baking in their spacious kitchens. This indifference was matched by a section of the NGO sector who would do nothing more than distributing food to long lines of migrants standing in the blazing sun of April-May, waiting for a basic charity meal. Many individuals did try to help, genuinely moved by the plight of the migrants, but there were also images of bright-looking young men and women taking selfies with the migrant workers to show their friends the good work they were doing doling out food. Then they went back to their zoom meetings and work-from-home comfort.

Residents of middle-class gated colonies forbade their maids from entering, masked or not, for fear that they may carry the virus, even though it was proven that this was a virus which had been spread by the rich travelling by air across continents. In all but a few cases, the maids got no salary, of course.

So, well-off Indians took to ordering food online. But even in these dire circumstances they did not forget their prejudices or let go of their hate. The media carried reports from different parts of the country of people refusing to accept food they had ordered on Zomato and other online sites because the delivery boys were Muslim. This level of bigotry and hatred is unprecedented in our history.

~

And yet, as I write this, it occurs to me that in our part of the world people have always been moved more by religious sentiments than by compassion for the poor and the oppressed, or the idea of justice.

During the 120 years of British rule in India, there were 120 devastating famines (in contrast, history records just 17 famines in the 2000 years before the British occupied the subcontinent). There were significant protests in some parts of the subcontinent, but the tragedy of these entirely avoidable famines did not unite the country. What did unite people and communities of almost all faiths to rise up against British imperialism was the revolt of 1857. And the immediate cause of this revolt, regarded as the largest and bloodiest uprising against European colonialism in the 19th century, was religious. In February 1857, new gunpowder cartridges were introduced for the Enfield rifles used by the Indian soldiers of the British army. The soldiers were required to tear open the cartridge paper with their teeth, and it was rumoured that the cartridges were greased with cow and pig fat. The British had offended the religious sensibilities of both Muslims and Hindus and united them in a massive uprising.

But for this single significant example, all others are about how religion and caste have always only divided us and created deep inequalities. Even our freedom fighters would not sit together and share a meal because they belonged to different castes and communities. In 1920, Mahatma Gandhi said that Hinduism does most emphatically discourage inter-dining and inter-marriage. He thought the restraint on inter-dining was essential for rapid development of the soul, conservation of certain social values and the cultivation of willpower.

But then he changed his mind and, in November 1932, he wrote: 'Restriction on inter-dining and inter-caste marriage is no part of the Hindu religion. It crept into Hinduism when perhaps it was in its decline.' Yet, despite what Gandhi had written, the idea of inter-dining was so offensive to upper-caste society that they were not willing even to hear of it. If anyone dared to challenge the caste system, there was the danger of a violent response from upper-caste Hindus.

In a letter dated 12 December 1935, the secretary of the Jat-Pat Todak Mandal (Society for the Abolition of the Caste System), a Hindu reformist organization based in Lahore, invited Baba Saheb Ambedkar to deliver a speech on the caste system in India at their annual conference in 1936. Ambedkar wrote the speech as an essay under the title 'Annihilation of Caste' and sent it in advance to the organizers in Lahore for printing and distribution. The organizers found many paragraphs provocative and wanted to delete them; Ambedkar declared in response that he 'would not change a comma'. The organizers then withdrew the invitation to him.

Ambedkar later explained in a letter why he differed with Gandhi on the efficacy of inter-dining and inter-marriage.

Here is the relevant passage:

> You also seem to be erring in the same way as the reformers working in the cause of removing untouchability. To agitate for

> and to organize inter-caste dinners and inter-caste marriages is like forced feeding brought about by artificial means. Make every man and woman free from the thraldom of the *Shastras*, cleanse their minds of the pernicious notions founded on the *Shastras*, and he or she will inter-dine and inter-marry without your telling him or her to do so.

These debates between Gandhi and Ambedkar are very relevant today in the context of beef bans and the imposition of vegetarianism.

The liberals have opposed the banning of beef and the promotion of vegetarianism largely on the ground that it violates the basic human right of an individual to choose what he or she wants to eat. However, the ban on beef is not merely a question of violation of individual civil liberties and human rights. The language of human rights is based on the primacy of an *individual's* right to liberty, dignity and equality. But when millions of people are *collectively* denied those human rights, then we need a stronger political discourse to challenge the deliberate exclusion of their cultures and communities.

The biggest achievement of the liberals in India was their right to food campaign. The campaign led to the passing of the National Rural Employment Guarantee Act in August 2005, the introduction of cooked mid-day meals in all primary schools following a Supreme Court order of April 2004, and finally the passing of the National Food Security Act, 2013. But even these achievements have been undermined by the controversies over beef and vegetarianism, which have served to divert public attention from the most fundamental issue: food security for the poor who cannot afford even one meal a day, and the wretched condition of farmers and their families, so many of whom have been driven to suicide.

Farmer suicides and the crisis in the agricultural sector are related to the globalization of the food industry and the so-called food safety laws that have been enacted by successive governments. These laws are also criminalizing the small dhabas and street vendors who provide affordable food to hundreds of millions of people. Some experts describe this as food fascism. And yet, there is silence in the mainstream media and among liberals about this.

~

When I began writing this introduction, farmers all over India had been protesting for several months against laws which they felt would bring big corporations into the agriculture sector and deprive farmers of control over their land, production and markets. The protest has been described as the largest organized strike in human history.

The protests began in November 2020. Farmers from Punjab, Haryana, UP and other parts of northern India spent the entire winter and then the harsh summer at the borders of Delhi, from where they were prevented by massive police presence, barricades, barbed wire and spikes from entering the Indian capital. The government refused to listen to their demands for over a year, until impending elections in some northern states forced it to withdraw the laws.

The protests took place in the background of the sharp decline in agricultural output from the late 1990s, and India has been moving from being a self-reliant nation with a food surplus to a net importer of food. I have been aware of these developments for over two decades in the context of the Northeast, especially Naga society. I saw people give up paddy cultivation because it was not economical; I saw fields being taken away for projects which led to the impoverishment of the local people. I saw how young people were giving up traditional diets and embracing fast food. I also saw how climate change was impacting agriculture.

Meanwhile, laws protecting tribal lands were being changed to allow big corporations to enter the sensitive ecological region.

~

Food anthropologists have demonstrated that hidden behind everyday foods are complex questions of power and status. For instance, Sidney W. Mintz's research demonstrated how Britain's insatiable sweet tooth was linked to the history of slavery, capitalism and imperialism.

In India, the growing craze for cakes and exotic desserts reflects the success of efforts to promote sugar consumption in the country by large sugar mills dealing with chronic oversupply—a problem of excess which stems partly from the huge incentives provided to growers in politically powerful rural areas.

The corporates and the politicians aligned with them decide what we grow, what we buy and what we eat. A visit to any shopping mall will show us the popularity of the 'food court', which is fast replacing street food. The noise in the malls drowns the protests by thousands of street hawkers who are being displaced by multi-national corporations such as Walmart. And our cuisines are being destroyed; our culinary imagination enslaved.

Under siege, the street food vendors are still holding on, keeping alive the rich diversities of our food culture. They also provide cheap food to millions of people. It is in the streets that we see the vibrancy of Indian people's daily struggles to survive, and that is why this book is dedicated to them.

This book tries to look at the issues of democracy, equality and justice through the lens of food—our food habits, preferences, rituals and taboos. By doing so, it is trying to keep alive the idea of an India which is as diverse, vibrant and exciting as our cuisines are. If it provokes us to think a little more about our prejudices and reflect on the everyday politics of food, we may yet live to know the taste of freedom.

NANDITA HAKSAR

December 2021

1

MEAT-EATING BRAHMINS FROM KASHMIR

I was born in London in 1954, the year rationing formally ended in Great Britain after it had been introduced during World War II. It was also the year that the first TV dinner appeared in the USA—the first step towards the appearance of junk food and the consequent obesity epidemic in that country.[1]

In India, where I grew up, fast food arrived much later and even when I was an undergraduate there were no diet fads, though there was a fetish about home-cooked food. And people who would be considered plump or fat today were looked upon as strong and healthy. I do not remember anyone going on a diet unless they had an upset stomach. Everyone in our community relished food rich in cholesterol and was sure that our cuisine was the best in the world, just as every other community in India celebrated theirs.

~

I belong to a community of meat-eating Brahmins—the Kashmiri Pandits. My ancestors came down from Kashmir sometime in the nineteenth century and settled in the plains of northern India. Very soon they forgot the culture, the rites and rituals and gradually even the language of the Kashmir Valley. The men learnt Urdu and Persian, while the women were taught Hindi and, on occasion, Sanskrit. The men greeted each other with an adaab-arz-hai, the women were always greeted with a namaskar.

The community did not have any collective memory of the life left behind in Kashmir. I never heard stories of any persecution which may have forced my ancestors to leave the beautiful Valley for the hot and dusty towns and cities of North India, which they always called Hindustan, to distinguish it from Kashmir. Most families had no links to their ancestral homes and never visited them, except perhaps as tourists.

Papa, my father, Parmeshwar Narain Haksar (1913–1998),[2] first visited Kashmir when he was in his fifties, and I went there with Papa's friend D.P. Dhar (1918–1975), who was a prominent politician and later, a diplomat. He was a very warm person and he took me with him to his home in Srinagar during my vacation from school. But once we got there, he left me to be looked after by his wife, Rani Bhabi, who showed her love by insisting on my drinking milk, which I did not like and which my mother had never insisted on my having. I found Uncle DP's home very feudal and there was almost nothing which made me identify myself with the culture or cuisine of Kashmiris living in the Valley.

~

Our community always called themselves 'Kashmiris' without any degree of self-consciousness. They even forgot that our Kashmiri food was not the same as the cuisine of the Kashmiris of the Valley. Even the Kashmiri Pandits in Kashmir would not recognize our cooking as being remotely Kashmiri, since our food had integrated many aspects of the cuisines of the plains, such as those of Lucknow, Allahabad and Delhi.

I had personally never felt 'Kashmiri'. If I was asked where I was from, I would say I was from Old Delhi. The Haksars had homes in the Walled City and had lived there for several generations. It was for this reason that I called myself a 'downstairs Kashmiri' to distinguish myself from the real Kashmiri-speaking Kashmiris from the Valley. Most of my family members could not understand this need to distinguish ourselves; in part because they did not know anything about Kashmir, its turbulent history or its cultural traditions. Most of us had never met any real Kashmiris.

The Kashmiri community living in the plains, in cities like Delhi, Lucknow and Simla, even had a Kashmiri Welfare Society which met regularly. The Society helped the members to keep in touch, provided a network for possible marriage alliances and occasionally celebrated festivals like Shivratri. The Society also possessed the special utensils needed to cook wedding feasts.

Papa, my father (above) and Amma, my mother (on the next page) with their parents and siblings.

~

In Kashmir, the most important festival for the Pandits is Shivratri. The celebrations last for several days. I read an account of Shivratri puja by a Kashmiri woman, Sudha Koul. I met Sudha in the early 1970s at a wedding and I still remember her, a vivacious woman singing Kashmiri songs. Sudha once wrote that 'being carnivorous was a survival tactic…and is deeply ingrained in our psyche as a metaphor for life, love and happiness'. She described a scene from one Shivratri she celebrated with her parents in Delhi:

> …grandfather would say with a resigned sigh, 'Okay, let's have lunch, and let's get it over with!' Even spiritual and religious old biddies felt no qualms in chomping on ear cartilage or marrow-bones long after the meal was done, pulverising everything into a heap on the thali. No one batted an eyelid.

No surprise then that even for Kashmiri Hindus (all Brahmins to a man or woman, no satisfactory explanation so far), the *prasad* offering at our most holy of holies, Shivratri *puja*, was a charger piled high with rice, cooked lamb and fish, and a luscious raw fish in its entirety atop the pile.

After wintering with my itinerant army parents, my grandparents fled the plains for the Valley every spring, frightened by the alien whir of the ceiling fan, and also [impelled] by the desire to celebrate Shivratri or Herath at home. One year, my father, posted as brigadier in Delhi Cantonment, persuaded his parents to stay with the lure that his regimental priest, a Sanskrit scholar, had promised to officiate. Thus it came to pass that we had the longest *puja pravachan*, or sermon, ever, and finally, to everyone's immense starving relief, the *prasad* was called for. My grandmother emerged proudly with her standard Shivratri platter held aloft and presented it to the *guruji*. He, obviously a ferocious vegetarian, stared at the raw fish, shell shocked, then instantaneously leapt to his feet and beat the hastiest retreat ever evidenced in those military precincts, shouting '*Traahi! Traahi! Traahi* (Help! Help! Help!)...'

My grandmother could not quite understand what she had done wrong. After all, she, and generations of Kashmiri Hindus, had taken whole raw lamb innards up to the goddess' shrines as sacred offerings. One piece lamb trachea, lungs, kidneys, liver, were ordered and sent uncut and un-detached by our Muslim butcher as per the centuries-old tradition, which he knew and respected well. Carried in covered wicker *krenjuls*, dripping with blood, these oblations were taken to Hari Parbat or Zeethyaar with pride and joy.[3]

We downstairs Kashmiris continued to celebrate Shivratri, even though Shiva is no longer the most important of the gods for the Kashmiri Pandits living in the plains. I remember that during my childhood most of our relatives had a breakfast of khatti kaleji or goat's liver in a sour gravy, which would shock the Shaivites of South India.

~

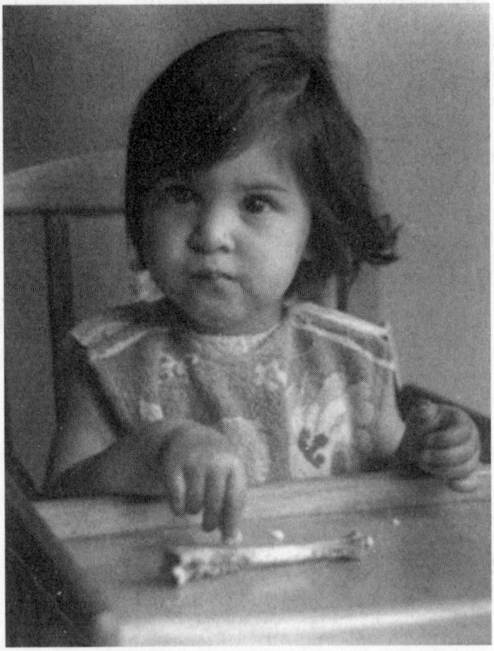

Meat-eater at age two.

My father was very proud of Kashmiri cuisine, especially the vast variety of meat dishes: rogan josh, pasandas, goli, koftas, kabargah, chuste (goat's intestines), gurde kapure (goat's kidney and testes), bheja or brain. In addition, there are many kinds of meat cooked with vegetables, such as turnips, called shabdegh; small meatballs cooked with methi (fenugreek), and meat cooked with knol-khol (kohlrabi).

In fact, there was even a dessert cooked with goat's meat called khubani, which means apricot. I remember tasting it at a wedding when I was a small child and the memory has stayed, not so much of the taste, but of the idea of a meaty dessert. I found the recipe in an old book by Krishna Prasad Dar (1893–1977). Krishna Prasad was an Indian printer and publisher. His printing press, Allahabad Law Journal Press, was one of the leading printers and publishers of the region. It was here that some of the books of Jawaharlal Nehru such as *Letters from a Father to His Daughter* and *Glimpses of World History* were published. Krishna Prasad's son, Sudhir Dar, the cartoonist, republished his book, *Kashmiri Cooking*, some years ago. Sudhir Dar does not exaggerate when he says: 'Each meal was an event, each dish a gourmet's delight and every day a royal feast.'

KHUBANI

The ingredients are the same as gulnar kebab except for the filling which is made up of:

Ingredients

- 1 kg sugar (for the syrup)
- 20 badams or kaju (almonds or cashews)
- 40 kishmish
- 300 gm ghee

Method

- In a karhai make a syrup of medium thick consistency with the sugar and four cups of water. If badams are used, soak them in hot water with the skin. Shape the meat in round balls as done for gulnar kebabs putting half a badam and one kishmish in the middle and fry the khubani till golden brown. Add the khubani into the syrup and let it rest.

I could not find the recipe for gulnar kebabs; a search on the Internet only showed up gulnar kebabs made with paneer, not meat. I have read that they originated in Persia, but the Kashmiris had improved on them by adding fenugreek leaves and pomegranate seeds.

~

Kashmiri cuisine, whether in the Valley or in the plains of Hindustan, is rich and we use ghee and mustard oil liberally and unashamedly. Not only is every dish made with a lot of ghee or mustard oil, but each ingredient is also deep-fried separately. So, for instance, if we make aloo-bhindi dum, the ladies fingers are first deep-fried and kept aside, then the potatoes are deep-fried and then the two are cooked together in ghee. The result is absolutely delicious.

I read an old recipe book written by a traditional Kashmiri chef in which he said that if the oil on top of the dish was not one finger deep, it was not a proper Kashmiri dish.

My mother, Urmila Haksar (1923-1989),[4] was fond of telling me the story of a guest at a Kashmiri wedding who went to wash his hands at the basin and when he was offered soap, said: 'The food was dry and there is no need for soap.' In other words: the food did not have enough chikanai or ghee, so soap was not required. That was the ultimate insult to the host—that the food was not rich enough.

The Kashmiris of the plains eat meat but we also consume vegetables, paneer and a variety of dals. And that is perhaps one of the significant differences between us downstairs Kashmiris and the Kashmiris who live in the Valley. I learnt this in 1973 at the wedding of my cousin, Arvind Kaul, who married a real Kashmiri-speaking Kashmiri from the Valley, Manmohini, then a research scholar at the Jawaharlal Nehru University. Arvind is the son of my mother's sister, whom I called Masi.

It was the day after the marriage ceremony when the bridegroom's family gives an important feast—the day non-vegetarian dishes are served. On the day of the actual marriage ceremony, since there is a puja, no non-vegetarian dishes are cooked. I arrived at Masi's home to find my new Kashmiri bhabi in tears. My aunt asked me to find out what had upset her daughter-in-law. It took a lot of persuasion to discover the reason. Manmohini confided that she had just learnt that we would only be serving four meat dishes at the feast, and we would also be serving dal. How would she show her face to her family; she was dying of embarrassment and shame! In Kashmir, they would make at least seven or eight meat dishes and never, ever serve yellow dal, even to ordinary guests, let alone at a wedding feast!

I myself had seen many relatives who could consume a kilo of meat in one sitting. But I had also seen the awful waste at weddings—though I believe our weddings have become less wasteful now.

~

It was during the wedding of Arvind and Manmohini that many of our family members came in contact with the Kashmiris of Kashmir. I believe that most of my family were blissfully unaware of the differences between our cuisine and that of the Pandits living in the Valley. A post on the blog of Vinayak Razdan, a Kashmiri-speaking Kashmiri Pandit, brought home the point rather dramatically.

He had posted the image of a bottle of mango chutney called Bichhua, saying: 'A product of Earthy Goods, this mango chutney with the catch line "a traditional Kashmiri recipe in memory

of Saraswati Mushran" presents an intriguing mystery. A Kashmiri recipe for mango chutney!'[5]

Obviously, mangoes are not native to Kashmir, so to call a mango chutney a 'traditional' Kashmiri recipe must seem odd to a Kashmiri from the Valley!

Saraswati Mushran was my father's older sister. She taught Linnet, her English daughter-in-law, the art of Kashmiri cooking. Many years after Saraswati Mushran died, Linnet bought my father's apple orchard in Himachal Pradesh and started making jams, just the way her German mother, Katherine, had taught her. The jams are famous as Bhuira jams—Bhuira is the name of the village where the orchard is situated. Among her famous jams and pickles is the aam ka bichhua—dedicated to the memory of Saraswati Mushran, her mother-in-law—which had so 'intrigued' Vinayak Razdan.

There was another Kashmiri tradition which my family honoured: the drying of vegetables in the sun before the onset of winter. My surname, Haksar, means people who dried haak—collard greens—for a living. In the severe cold winters of Kashmir the dried vegetables would have come in handy, but in Delhi vegetables were easily available all the year around. Yet, the downstairs Kashmiris continued the practice of drying vegetables: shaljams (a kind of turnip), radishes, knol-khol, cabbage, cauliflower and some special greens. I still remember climbing up the eighty-three steps to Masi's flat overlooking Janpath to find her and her mother-in-law busy drying vegetables on the terrace. At the time I did not find it strange.

There are a wide variety of vegetarian dishes in Kashimiri Pandit cuisine, including chaaman or paneer, dry sabzis, and vegetables in gravy. The vegetables are categorized as sweet—cauliflower, peas, carrots, cabbage—and salty—vegetables such as brinjal, okra, potatoes, greens like spinach and the leaves of knol-khol or haak. According to our tradition, sweet vegetables could be cooked together but never combined with salty; for instance, we would never cook cauliflower with bitter gourd or okra with cabbage. The salty vegetables were often cooked with tomatoes or green mango powder, aamchur. We never use tamarind.

Our staple food is rice, cooked to ensure that each grain is separate. We had rice twice a day, but over time and under the influence of our neighbours in the plains, we downstairs Kashmiris did start having phulkas or rotis.

~

Kashmiri Pandits did not traditionally eat onions or garlic, either in their raw form or cooked, and in the old days, even tomatoes were forbidden. Instead, we use yoghurt and hing—called devil's dung by the Germans! This gave Kashmiri Pandit cuisine its distinct flavours, in contrast to the Kashmiri Muslim cuisine.

Onions and garlic are supposed to stimulate our baser instincts and are not part of the satvic diet of Brahmins. In my childhood I do not remember ever eating onions or garlic either at home or at the homes of relatives. Apparently neither the four Vedas nor the sixteen Upanishads mention the onion. When the onion does appear in Aryan writings, 'It is as a food of the despised native population, the mlecchas, and of foreigners (yavanas), to be shunned by those seeking an austere life, as well as on ceremonial occasions.'[6]

I remember my mother telling me how food was divided

into satvic for Brahmins, rajasic for the Kshatriyas and tamasic for the lower castes. Although my parents did not practice caste discrimination and did not have separate utensils for the sweepers, as we called them, they, like other Kashmiri Brahmin families, looked down upon the onion and garlic till many years later, when both the vegetables became part of our everyday cooking. However, that did nothing to make us aware of how deeply Brahminism had seeped into our cultural outlook.

I do not remember the same prejudice against the tomato, but many Kashmiri Pandits from the older generation did not eat it because it was a vegetable that came from across the seas. The tomato originated in Mexico but came to India with the English around the 1850s. It is not an essential ingredient in Kashmiri Pandit cooking.

Amma, my mother, gave me my first lessons in eating etiquette: never eat with the left hand; while eating, make sure no more than the tips of the fingers are used to make a luqma (a mouthful) and then put it into the mouth with the aid of the thumb. Under no circumstances should the palm have food on it. I wonder what she would have said if she knew that these rules have been elaborated on and illustrated on the internet, for example, by WikiHow: How to Eat Indian Food with your Hands in Six Steps.

More importantly, Amma did not realize that much of this etiquette was based on caste rules of purity and pollution. So, even though we did break many caste rules and taboos, this teaching made me a cultural Brahmin, if not a religious one. But all this I discovered much, much later.

Papa taught me to make tasty luqmas. Take a bit of rice, and then wet it with dal or the gravy of the meat, add a bit of the vegetable and then mix it all well so each mouthful is artfully blended to produce a burst of flavour in the mouth. The most delicious luqmas could be made only after the bowl was empty and the grease of the gravy remained. Then I was allowed to put in rice and wipe the bowl clean, mixing the meat gravy with the rice. Sometimes Papa would tease me by pretending to take away the luqma I had kept for the last, and sometimes we shared our luqmas. Amma watched the scene and saw the delight in my eyes but she never shared her food—she just could not eat jootha or impure food, even from her daughter's plate. I teased her about her Brahmanical habits—little realizing how these pernicious traditions had seeped into our subconscious so insidiously with every luqma.

Amma also taught me how a meal must be balanced. I don't mean from the point of view of the nutritionist, but according to the tradition of balancing flavours in our cuisine. If two meat dishes were to be cooked, then one would be with chunks of meat or sabut meat, and the other with minced meat. The vegetables would have to be matched with the kind of meat being cooked. We always serve dals, even at weddings, because they offset the richness of the meat dishes.

There was one other thing that I was taught: Kashmiri Pandits do not taste the food during the cooking; it would be considered jootha. Amma taught me how to blow the steam from the pot towards my nose and smell it in order to decide whether the salt was enough. The steam had to be blown towards the nose so that I would not directly sniff the dish, for that too would make it jootha. Of course, if I had done it no one in our home would have thrown the food away; but it was something I had observed from my childhood. That is how I unknowingly imbibed Brahmanism in my being. Even today, when I watch celebrity cooks on TV tasting their dishes as they cook, I find myself cringing.

~

The relative I was most fond of was my Dada. He was not my father's father, who had died in 1944, ten years before I was born. Dada was Rajinder Narain Haksar (1893–1982), or Inder Bhai, as most people called him.

Dada was tall and walked upright. He had a moustache and smoked cigars from wooden boxes. He always wore white kurtas which were starched; the sleeves were crinkled by the dhobi in the traditional style. He was a patron of the arts and had helped set up the Bharatiya Kathak Kendra.

He was the first one in the Haksar family to open a shop. Trading was considered a profession for the Bania caste, not Brahmins. Dada, like his two older brothers, had studied law, but he had more varied interests, such as music and poetry, which earned him a reputation of being an awaara or vagabond. In 1929 he opened a cloth shop in Lahore and called it Pandit Brothers. But after the Partition of India he rented a shop in Chandini Chowk, within the Walled City, and later, two shops in F Block of Connaught Place.

A case was filed against Pandit Brothers in 1954, the year I was born. The Income Tax officer found that the shops did not make enough profit. But in the appeal, the court found that even though the shops did not make profit and did not seem to be run on business principles, there were no illegalities or irregularities. In that judgement the judge observed:

> The expense ratio was very high. The employees appear to be paid not exactly on business-like principles—there appear to be a lot of philanthropic motives behind the very high payments made to them which are disproportionate to their qualifications and the nature of work done by them. They would not be able to get anywhere near the remunerations which the assessee is paying to them anywhere else in the open market. Only those

> expenses are allowable which can be brought down to strictly business principles. Philanthropy and business are strangers.[7]

The judge did not know that apart from his generosity to his employees, whom he considered family, Dada's other non-business-like expenses included the money he spent hosting poets, singers and artists who visited him regularly and even stayed in his home. I remember Dada sitting in his shop surrounded by poets, singers and musicians, entertaining them and enjoying animated debates on the meaning of Urdu or Persian words in a poem or ghazal. Behind him in the shop were dozens of Urdu, English and Persian dictionaries which were pulled out during these animated discussions.

Dada

Whenever I visited Dada, he would give me a small Cadbury chocolate wrapped in blue paper. If I remember correctly, it cost five paise. I specially remember the visits to his shop in Chandini Chowk before he started sitting in his Connaught Place shop. Dada never ate food bought from the bazaar. It was Amma who took me to the famous jalebiwala near the Pandit Brothers shop in Chandini Chowk. The man-made oversized jalebis called jalebas. The joy of biting into a hot, juicy sweet cannot be described adequately in words. I believe the man's sons still stand outside Dariba selling the jalebas which have become famous.

And then there was the sohan halwa from Ghantewale's sweet shop, which was opened in 1790. It is said that Mughal emperors bought sweets from Ghantewala, and there are even stories about the rebels who took part in the war of independence in 1857 claiming that Ghantewala's sweets were among the wonders of Delhi. Bollywood celebrated the shop in a film called *Chandini Chowk* in 1954, but in 2015 the shop was closed down due to various legal entanglements. And around 2015, the Chandini Chowk branch of Pandit Brothers was also sold off and I did not even know that it was gone.

Nearby was the goli or marble sodawala. Amma loved the lemon drink sold in thick glass bottles with marbles as stoppers. In order to 'open' the bottle you pushed the marble down till it went inside the bottle, and then you could drink straight from it. I can't say I took to the drink, but the pushing down of the marble was exciting indeed. Baab Mallya from Mangalore, who also remembers this wonder bottle with fondness, writes:

> Remember the days when soda was sold in goli bottles? I used to enjoy drinking from them but most importantly, loved to hear the sound as it was opened. There were a couple of ways

Street vendor selling lemon soda

> to open it, one with a wooden device with a central projection which pushed the marble back inside the bottle and the other with the finger!
>
> Typically, the bottle was pressed against the shoulder as it was opened. At times it was frustrating for me as a kid to drink because the marble kept [blocking the neck of the bottle]. Until one day as I was looking at the empty bottle, turning it around, holding it upside down, I realized that in certain positions the marble got locked into place.
>
> Poured water into the bottle and tried my newly acquired knowledge; my excitement and thrill of this discovery was too much to contain.[8]

Dada ate only Kashmiri food. He did not eat onions and garlic. This was not a religious belief, but because he believed that Kashmiri food without garlic and onions had a superior taste. He ate traditional, rich Kashmiri food, with at least one meat dish cooked slowly to perfection, every single day of his life till the very end. Dada, like most Kashmiris living in the plains, did not exercise or diet. They ate their rich Kashmiri food and served it proudly.

He died on the morning of 2 January 1982 while shaving and instructing his cook, Moti, on how to ensure the raan was perfectly cooked for the guests who would be coming for dinner. Dada had trained Moti and he was one of the best cooks within our family.

What a wonderful way to go.

~

In honour of Dada's memory I give you the recipe of the famous raan, cooked the Kashmiri Pandit way. Many Kashmiri Pandits add onions and even garlic, but Dada remained steadfast to tradition:

RAAN

Ingredients

- 1 kg haunch of goat (remove all white membranes and fat)
- 4 heaped tbsp yoghurt
- 250 gm mixed ghee and mustard oil
- 1 pinch hing

For raan masala

- 1 tbsp khas-khas (poppy seeds)
- 4 whole Kashmiri mirch, de-seeded and soaked
- 1 small piece raw coconut
- 50 gm peeled fresh ginger
- 4 pieces cinnamon
- 3 badi elaichi
- 8 chhoti elaichi
- 2 cloves
- 2 nutmegs
- 2 heaped tbsp saunf
- 2 tsp zeera powder
- 2 tsp Kashmiri red chilli powder
- 4 bay leaves
- 1 tsp salt

Method

- Grind masala ingredients together finely but not too wet, and set aside. Stab raan with fork repeatedly until meat becomes completely loose. Using hands, rub in two heaped tbsp yoghurt and one tsp salt. Spread the masala and continue stabbing meat for a total of about 40 minutes. Tie the raan securely with narrow cotton strips to keep the meat on bone. Leave in fridge overnight.
- To cook, heat large degchi, and put in the ghee and oil. Dissolve hing in three tbsp water and add to degchi. Beat

two tbsp yoghurt and add. Place raan carefully in degchi. Cover and weight lid. Use low fire. Periodically spoon oil and masala over raan; don't allow masala to stick.

- Flip raan carefully to brown evenly. Add a little water at a time and baste until well cooked and tender. When done, place on platter and remove cloth strips. Pour remaining masala over raan. The meat should be tender enough to spoon off the bone.

~

In my childhood I remember we were always going to parties at the homes of various relatives and there was a good deal of excitement at the prospect of having a hearty Kashmiri meal. I do not think these parties were thrown on special occasions, such as birthdays or wedding anniversaries. That was not a part of our traditional culture. I think it was more a celebration of the cuisine. And the talk also revolved around food, cooking, the pros and cons of using a pressure cooker. In fact, until 1970, when I started going to college, our food was still cooked on coal fires, although we had a gas stove. Kashmiri cooking requires the cook to stand for long hours by the stove to ensure the meat does not get burnt as it roasts for a minimum of an hour.

My mother's masi, Shanno Nani, used an Anand Cooker which allowed slow cooking without the cook being present all the time. Anand Cookers are still available in Old Delhi and they come in different shapes

Shanno Nani

and sizes. It was basically an insulated tiffin carrier with a stove at the bottom, so food could be both cooked and carried. I was delighted to find this account of one by Vikram Doctor, who writes:

> A couple of months back, this column looked at a piece of kitchen equipment called the Santosh Cooker. A pamphlet from the 1950s, picked up from a friend, described what seemed to be an insulated tiffin carrier with a stove at the bottom, so food could be both conveniently cooked and carried around. I ended by asking if any readers knew more about this device.
>
> And did they ever! Arun Khanna remembers watching with awe as a child as his grandfather put raw food into the containers, blew on the coals and checked on the food every 40 minutes to see if it was done. His mother and grandmother were most appreciative, he says, 'Because during the time they had a gala reprieve from the kitchen...'[9]

My Shanno Nani would have agreed about the Anand Cooker being 'a gala reprieve from the kitchen'. The reprieve allowed her to listen to cricket commentaries which she had a quiet passion for.

~

Of course, the best Kashmiri food was found at weddings when a professional cook was employed. But these traditional Kashmiri weddings are all a distant dream for me. The first one I remember, but not in great detail, was the wedding of my father's younger brother, Krishan Kumar Haksar, with Roop Zutshi in May of 1957. I was barely three years old and the memories I have of that occasion are not of the Kashmiri food, but of my first box of biscuits.

Roop Chachi lived in Simla and so our family went there for the wedding ceremony. At the time my pupha, K.P. Mushran

Krishan Chacha and Roop Chachi just after their wedding

(Saraswati Mushran's husband), was a member of the Railway Board and entitled to a saloon, which was a specially manufactured coach with bedrooms, drawing room and a fully equipped kitchen. I remember the carpeted drawing room with its wooden furniture. The most exciting part was the bell which could be rung and, as if by magic, a liveried waiter would appear, ready to fulfil my every wish! Now tourists can travel in saloon cars on luxury trains, such as the Palace on Wheels, at a cost of fifty thousand to five lakh rupees per person per journey!

When we reached Simla, we stayed in the railway guest house and there my Chachi's parents came, quiet and dignified. Her mother gifted me biscuits in a tin with a painting on the lid. When I opened the box I could not believe the variety of biscuits I saw: there were thin, long pink wafers, crisp rectangular biscuits sprinkled with sugar, round biscuit sandwiches with orange cream and, my favourite, round biscuits filled with red sticky jam with holes in the middle!

When I phoned Chachi to check the date of her wedding, she told me that it was at her marriage that she was presented a pressure cooker by Saraswati's daughters, Indu, Kunti and Madhu. Till then she had never seen a pressure cooker.

She said she had seen a grinder in Chandigarh before her marriage. One of her father's friends had got it from abroad. Then she asked my father, who was posted in London in the 1960s, to bring her an electrical grinder, and he had brought her one in 1964. Chachi remembered how my father had taught her to use the grinder by grinding moong ki daal and they had made small delicate moong ki pakoris.

~

The wedding I remember most vividly is the wedding of my mother's younger brother, Shashi Sapru, in Lucknow. It was in 1966, long after my maternal grandparents had died.

My maternal grandparents, Dinanath and Chuni Sapru, were a part of the Kashmiri community that lived in Lucknow. Most of the Kashmiris lived in the Kashmiri Mohalla, but Nana had a home on Faizabad Road. The Kashmiris of Lucknow considered themselves much more cultured and civilized since they had absorbed many of the manners and etiquette of this town so famous for its good manners and polished language.

Nani and Nana were gentle souls; at least that is how I remember them. I do not have a single bad memory of them. But Amma says Nana once slapped her when she served mangoes without peeling them. Amma was a young woman, and this kind of violence was not at all common. But she had committed a serious violation of Lucknowi etiquette by serving the mangoes without first peeling them.

Amma, too, would not tolerate mangoes being eaten without peeling them; and she got seriously upset if Papa sucked the pulp directly from the mango. If my father were caught sucking a mango she would explain his bad manners were due to the fact that he was from Allahabad, not Lucknow. Besides, he had been brought up in the jungles of the Central Provinces!

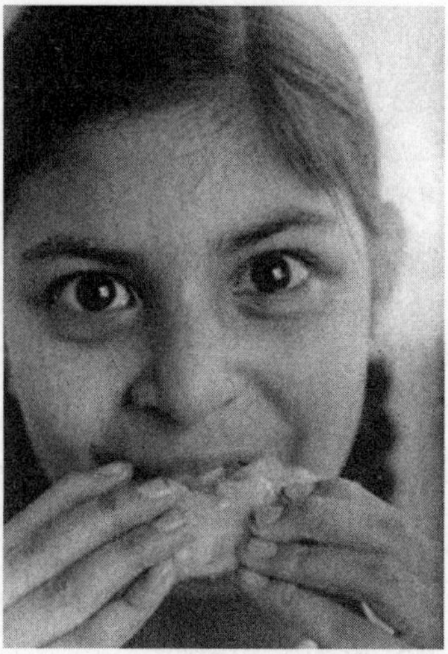

Eating a safeda

There was no doubt in my mother's mind that the best mangoes were Dussehri, Langra and Chausa. No other mango qualified to be put on our table. The only mango one was allowed to suck was the small Safeda, because it was too fibrous to be sliced.

Amma even peeled grapes. Adani Mao, a Naga friend from Manipur, once asked me what was so special about Lucknowi culture; he had heard it was something special and wanted to experience it. And the first thing that came to my mind was that people in Lucknow ate meat in the form of exquisite melt-in-the-mouth kebabs, and de-seeded grapes before putting them in their mouths. When I told Adani this, he looked at me in utter disbelief.

I remembered the old saying that the begums of Lucknow were so delicate that their feet got blistered when walking on velvet... but none of this could convey the uniqueness of Lucknawi culture to a Naga. Then I explained: 'Lucknow culture is known for its poets and extremely polite way of speaking and its etiquette.' Adani smiled. That he understood. Nagas put a premium on politeness.

Amma was by no means intolerant. But she did consider Lucknawi culture to be vastly superior to Punjabi culture and cuisine. She deeply resented the invasion of Delhi by Punjabi culture and its creeping influence even in UP. She would complain bitterly that everywhere, chhole bhature were taking over puri and aloo sabzi; fruit chaat seemed to be replacing the traditional chaat and shakes were replacing sherbets.

Once Amma took me to the Chowk area of Lucknow. We stopped for a paan and I asked for a sweet paan. The paanwala very gently said: 'Bitiya, you won't get meetha paan *here*.' Sweet paan has a blob of gulkand, a jam made of roses, sweet betel nuts and peppermint.

Amma was not gentle: 'Meetha paan is eaten only by Punjabis. We in Lucknow do not eat it.'

~

I remember so many of the women in our family sitting with their silver paan daans, special boxes with a tray for the leaves and beneath it, several compartments for the accessories such as lime, kattha, betel nuts. Papa's sister would sit chatting with Dadi while cutting the betel nut into fine pieces—the click-click of the sarota or betel-cutter was soothing to my ears. My Dadi insisted that my father had a dark complexion because she ate too much kattha when she was pregnant with him.

Perhaps the best celebration of the paan is by Amir Khusro (1253–1325) in his book *Ijaaz-e-Khusravi* where he speaks of its qualities. Amir Khusro was a Sufi musician, poet and scholar and is considered the father of qawwali. He is buried in Delhi's Nizamuddin dargah.

Qualities of the paan

1. Prophet Mohammad (peace be upon Him) has informed us about its benefit.
2. It fortifies the roots of the teeth and it is known by experience that the teeth of the inhabitants of other lands fall because of eating fruits while the [teeth of Indians] who use [paan] do not fall.
3. It removes the pus in teeth which is a source of abhorrence, and it brightens teeth.
4. Removes the foul smell of the mouth.
5. When it is chewed it produces a good smell, which [makes] the mind of those present fragrant.
6. It removes phlegm.
7. Makes the heart cheerful.
8. All fats are source of redness, and this leaf removes redness.
9. For the healing of the wound of arrow or sword, it is tied on the wound.
10. It prevents vomiting and [eases] heart burning.
11. For the satiated it increases appetite.
12. It is a source of satiety in hunger.
13. It brings a little intoxication.
14. Of the nine tastes, it has three perfect ones—bitter, salty and Sweet—and tasteless pungent.
15. Six fruits have six different tastes while this leaf tastes as if it is all the six fruits.
16. Of the seven colours, it has five perfect ones—red, green, white, blackish like aloe wood, and yellow.
17. [It is never] without companions—areca nut, lime, and colour.
18. Everywhere fruits are eaten and not the leaf but here the leaf is taken as a fruit.
19. Monarchs never keep any food in the robe except [paan] and that too with great honour.

20. Eating anything in a market is regarded a bad habit but this food is a sign of greatness.
21. It is used on the occasion of entertainment, it is always kept away from mourning and grief.
22. It is fit for hospitality.
23. All the leaves separated from the branch do not survive beyond one day, while this leaf is fresh even after six months.
24. It is fresh with water and also fresh without water.
25. By taking the betel the beauty of the handsome person increases.
26. It turns pearl-like teeth into the sun-faced Indian (women's gem.
27. It decorates the assembly of companions.
28. Of the gifts that are exchanged between the lover and the beloved, none is better than this.
29. Its taste is [blissful] and not sensual.
30. Its external form is admirable.[10]

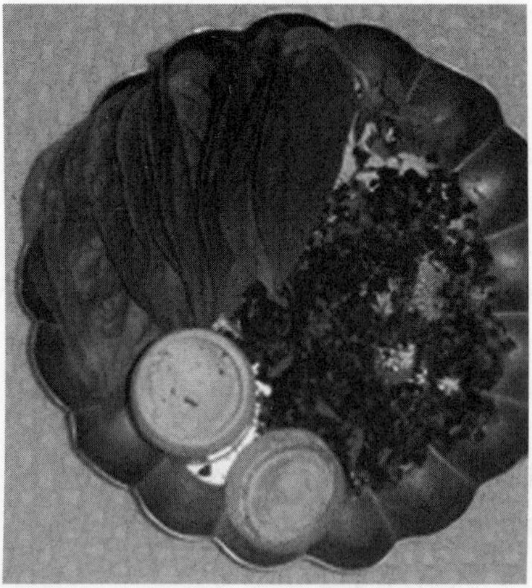

Paan leaves, supari, kattha

Amma would have pointed out that Amir Khusro does not mention sweet paans. You can have one or the other, according to purists—a paan, or a sweet, you do *not* mix the two. And a paan is always superior to a sweet. In fact, paan seems to have been more important than sweets even a thousand years ago, if we go by Alberuni's description of Diwali in his *Tahkik-i-Hind* written in 1030 AD:

> The first *Karttika*, or new moon's day, when the sun marches in Libra, is called Dibali. Then people bathe, dress festively, make presents to each other of betel-leaves and areca-nuts; they ride to the temples to give alms and play merrily with each other till noon. In the night they light a great number of lamps in every place so that the air is perfectly clear…

Amma would have been truly horrified to learn that Delhi's famous Prince Paan's Om Prakash Lalwani introduced flavoured paan in his Daryaganj shop, including chocolate, pineapple and mogra flavours. There is a paan parlour in Delhi which sells paan in forty-one flavours, among them a 'honeymoon paan' wrapped in gold-leaf and stuffed with dry fruits and nuts.

~

My memories of Lucknow are full of warmth. The train from Delhi arrived early in the morning and by the time our tonga had clip-clopped to Faizabad Road it was time for breakfast. I would run to the waiting arms of my grandparents. Even while hugging me my grandfather would call out: 'Ganesh, Nandiji has come. Bring hot jalebis.' Ganesh would walk down from Nana's house, past IT College where my mother and her sister had studied, to the crossing where there was a shop and return with hot jalebis. Perhaps it was the feeling of being truly welcomed, the warmth of the reception and the dignity of being called 'Nandiji' that made the hot, syrupy jalebis taste divine.

Apparently, jalebi is a corruption of the Arabic zalabiyah or Persian zoolbia. In school I learnt that in Punjab they had jalebis in the evenings. Once, when I told my mother that the girls in my boarding school said their mothers gave them jalebis with hot milk, she replied very firmly: 'They must be Punjabi. We don't have our jalebis in milk; it would make them soggy.' I never did like milk, so I had no reason to disagree.

Amma introduced me to another kind of jalebi when we went to visit relatives in Calcutta (long before it became Kolkata): a jalebi made with Bengali soft cheese or chhena. Many years later, when I was teaching in Cochin, a friend told me that the Muslims of Kerala made a kind of jalebi called muttamala with egg yolks. Egg yolk is filled into a coconut shell with a single hole and then poured into boiling sugar syrup. When done, the jalebi or muttamala is laid on a snow-white pudding made of egg whites called pinnanathappam.

~

In the evening in Lucknow, the servants would bring out large and noisy pedestal fans and place the rattan chairs in the garden which had been watered. Then my grandparents' guests would arrive; the women in pastel shades of crisp chikankari-embroidered saris and the men in crisp white cotton kurtas and churidars—the sleeves of their kurtas skilfully crinkled by the dhobi. (It is said that Nur Jehan, the wife of Mughal Emperor Jehangir, introduced chikanwork in Lucknow and the original embroidery was always white on white.) The guests would be served sherbet made from seasonal fruits, such as purple phalsa or aam ka panna. The Lucknow aam ka panna had a smoky taste because the mangoes were roasted on coals instead of being boiled.

I don't remember what the conversations were about, but there was a lot of reciting of Urdu poems and laughter. Among the famous poets of Lucknow was Anand Narain Malla (1901–1997). He won the Sahitya Akademi award in Urdu in 1964 for his poetry, specifically the book *Meri Hadis-e-Umr-e-Gurezan*. He was also a recipient of the Iqbal Samman, a prestigious literary award, at age ninety-two. Amma told me that Nandoo Bhai, as we called him, would sometimes recite his poems in the Coffee House in Lucknow. When people heard that he was reciting they would pour in to listen. He challenged the idea that Urdu was the language of the Muslims alone. He said if that were so, he would change his religion. In 1967 he was elected to the Lok Sabha as an Independent candidate from the Lucknow constituency.

Nandoo Bhai's wife was Annapoorna, whose father and Nana's mother were siblings. Nandoo Bhai and Annapoorna Bua's love story was famous. It was said she was so beautiful that both Anand and his brother fell in love with her and when she married Anand, the brother left for England and stayed there, preferring to remain a bachelor all his life.

I used to meet Nandoo Bhai in the corridors of the Supreme Court where he practiced after retiring as a judge from the Allahabad High Court, where he served from 1954 to 1961. His observations on the UP police force in *State vs Mohammad Naim (Criminal Misc. Case No. 87 of 1961)* are still widely quoted by judges and human rights activists: '...there is not a single lawless group in the whole of the country whose record of crime comes anywhere near the record of that organised unit which is known as the Indian Police Force.'

~

I never had an opportunity to listen to any poetry reading sessions in the Coffee House of Lucknow but I do remember the wonderful tea parties we had in Kwality restaurant. On every visit to Lucknow, Amma's uncle (her mother's mamu's son), Suraj Kichilu, would invite us for a tea party at 5 p.m. The excitement of going to Kwality was topped by the anxiety of being on time because Suraj Mamu was a stickler for punctuality. He arrived in style in his 1936 Ford VH on the dot of five and woe to anyone who turned up even a minute late!

I have always loved tea parties because we could have such a variety of food—pastries, shammi kebabs or meat cutlets, sandwiches, shakes and ice cream, especially the tutti-frutti served in a tall glass.

And then came the grand finale—as we stood watching, Suraj Mamu's driver would insert the crank handle and start the car!

The last time I went to Kwality restaurant was when we had gone to attend my Mamu's wedding. It was the last family gathering in Lucknow. This was in 1966. By then my mother's parents, Nana and Nani, were dead. But we all gathered together in their old house on Faizabad Road. Amma was in charge because Masi had not come as she had recently become a widow.

It was also one of my last train journeys in the old-fashioned way when we carried masses of luggage; large and heavy suitcases without any thought or worry about the size or weight. And the green holdalls with our bedding, pillows all rolled up and tied with leather straps. These we unrolled at night. Most people carried their own food and it was usually puri aloo or paratha aloo. But my mother said it was much more fun to try the different kinds of savouries and sweets available at each station.

This was why I loved the train journeys, simply because we would eat at every station. Amma would be at the window telling me what the speciality of each town was: Agra ka angoori petha, Mathura ka peda, Sandile ke ladoo and so on. Besides, these was the hot, sweet tea served in earthenware cups, though neither my mother nor I had any inkling of their ecological significance. For me, it was fun to throw the cup out and watch it break into smithereens.

Amma even enjoyed the railway food, especially the BBT (bread-butter-tea) with vegetable cutlets offered for breakfast. Now the trains whiz past, not stopping at the smaller stations; the variety has been substituted by Indian Railway's institutionalized food and the latest news is that the food is substandard.

Mamu had a proper Kashmiri wedding which lasted four or five days. The women sat together peeling, shelling and cutting the vegetables while poor Amma tried her best to do a crash course as event manager.

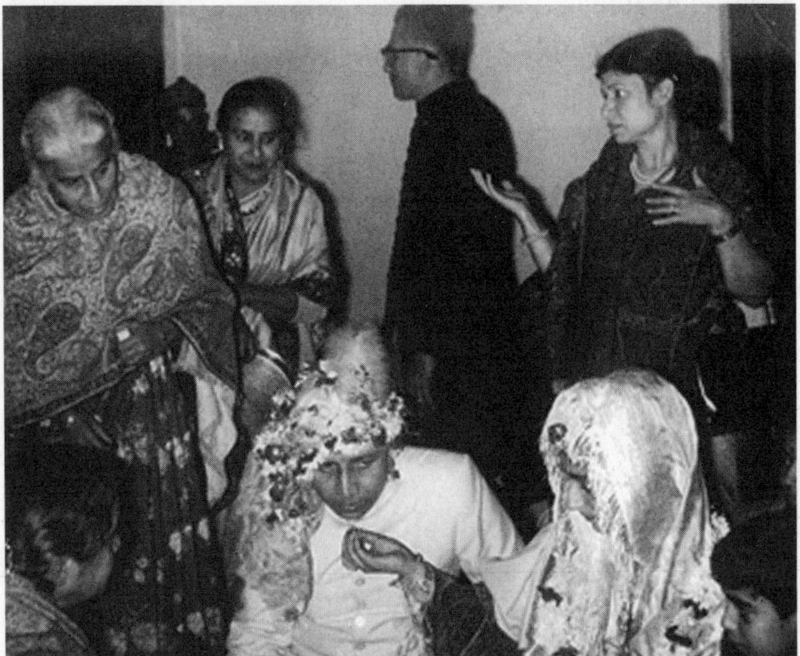

Mamu's wedding

The first thing that had to be done was to make baris with lentils and spices, each with a hole in the middle. They were sun-dried and were delicious when added to various vegetables and cooked with a sour gravy, or khhatti sabzi.

The baris were distributed among relatives along with gota—a mixture of grated coconut and flakes of almonds and pistachios—and a packet of attahroo or athoor. All the three items were put in small handmade purses with drawstrings and given to near relatives.

The attahroo or athoor was a string, usually red in colour, with gold tassels, which was gifted to relatives on every wedding. A Kashmiri bride is given a hexagonal gold ear ornament by her mother which is attached to a string put through a hole in the upper ear cartilage. Later, her in-laws put another string—the attahroo or athoor.

At Mamu's wedding the breakfasts were my favourite meals. The wedding breakfasts consisted of such delicacies as khameeri puri made from fermented dough with meetha dahi, sweet yoghurt whipped smooth and flavoured with cardamom and served in earthenware cups. Then there was a bread, more like a cake, called sheermaal, which was toasted and eaten with lots of butter; goat's liver; and, of course, the frothy nimish which epitomizes the famed culture of Lucknow. This frothy, light sweet has both nazaakat and nafaasat (delicacy and neatness—though these are both inadequate translations). This is what I found about nimish on the Internet:

> *Makhan Malai* and *Nimish* have become synonymous but few know that there is a minor difference between the two. While the former originated in India using cow's milk, the latter is an Afghani dessert in which horse's milk was used. But the method is almost the same...in both *Makhan Malai* and *Nimish*, the mixture of milk, cream and sugar is hung in a clay pot all

> night under the winter sky. The peculiar freshness and lightness comes from a dollop of dew, the secret ingredient added to it by Mother Nature. Early every morning, the clay pot is taken off the peg and the mixture is blended using a *mathaani* (manual wooden blender), to make it frothy.[11]

I am sure Amma would not have believed that nimish was originally made from horse's milk. It would have offended her Lucknowi sensibility.

The very last time I had nimish was in the 1970s. It was then I learnt that in Old Delhi they called it daulat ki chaat. I believe it is still available if you phone Kemchand Adesh Kumar at 9899417485 (at least this was the case at the time of writing this book). He can be found at Nai Sarak on early winter mornings. But he says that after him there may not be anybody to continue the traditional way of preparing it.

That is not true. There are efforts to keep alive the memory of this dish, but in ways Amma may not have approved of. For instance, Priti Narain has a recipe for daulat ki chaat in *The Essential Delhi Cookbook*, in which she calls it 'milk puff'. My father would certainly not approve of that translation and would have dismissed the recipe as a 'fraud' because it prescribes the use of an electric mixer! Here is Priti's recipe:

DAULAT KI CHAAT

Ingredients

- 2 litres full cream milk, unboiled
- 2 and a quarter cups cream
- 1 heaped tsp cream of tartar
- 1 cup caster sugar
- 1 tsp rosewater
- 2 tbsp chopped pistachio nuts

Method

- Combine milk, cream and cream of tartar in a large bowl and refrigerate overnight.
- Next morning stir in 4 tsp caster sugar and rosewater and whisk using a rotary or electric beater at high speed. Using a tea strainer collect the foam that forms and transfer to a large thali or tray. Keep thali tilted so that foam stays on one side; some milk will collect on the lower side. When the thali is fairly full, spoon foam into clay saucers or teacups, sprinkling a little caster sugar between layers and on top (the foam will condense a little during this operation. What looks like four bowlfuls in the thali will yield only two bowls).
- Pour milk collected in the thali back in the bowl and continue collecting foam till all the milk is used up. The whole process will take 2–2.5 hours.
- Sprinkle pistachio nuts on top of each bowl of foam and refrigerate till serving time.
- The daulat ki chaat can also be layered in 2–3 large bowls but it loses some of its fluffines and becomes dense.

I have read that the celebrity cook Manish Malhotra also makes daulat ki chaat and it is on his menu at his restaurant, Indian Accent, in Delhi. My parents would have been truly horrified, as was I when I read that this ethereal dish was described as 'seminal gastronomical foam' on the Internet. But perhaps nimish will survive because it has found other patrons—foreign embassies!

~

Before leaving Lucknow, Amma and I would take a rickshaw to Ram Asrey's sweet shop, open since 1805, to buy sweets for relatives back in Delhi. The most famous sweet at the shop was and is the balai ki gilori, or malai ka paan as the non-Lucknowites call it. It is a sweet as delicate and ephemeral as the nimish. The original balai ki gilori had a paper-thin malai in which were stuffed mishri crystals with a hint of rosewater and kewra and covered by silver varq. As Chef Ranveer Brar says: 'The beauty of our balai ki gilori is its melt-in-the-mouth quality and its delicate taste, especially the one with kesar ki mishri.' Ram Asrey continues to thrive to this day.

But it was not balai ki gilori that we took back with us to Delhi, because it would not have survived the train journey and the heat. Our favourites were the bhuna pedas, which are called 'red pedas'.

~

In the summers, Dadi would insist that my sister and I carry raw onions with us and sniff them to prevent getting a heat stroke. Amma did not contradict her mother-in-law, but she made it plain that she did not think highly of such traditional remedies.

And yet, although Amma always said rather vehemently that she did not believe in the traditional medical systems, she was the one who passed on her knowledge of home remedies which have turned out to be useful.

Amma told me about hot and cold foods. It is not as if she had sat me down one day and explained ayurveda, but over the years I had picked up the notion that foods are divided into hot and cold. I had no idea that the hot–cold concept was the basis of ancient Indian medical knowledge and that it spread through Arabic translations of medical texts written by Indian doctors Manka and Saleh; and was then translated into Greek and then Spanish. Thus, it is said, the theory also became a part of medical teachings in Mexico and South America.[12]

I knew that if I got loose motions I should not have hot foods such as mangoes. I also knew that the antidote to eating too many mangoes was milk; and that one should not drink water after eating fruits. So, if I have a stomach upset I have cold foods such as khichdi with dahi or yoghurt. But if khichdi is made as a meal, then it should be accompanied by its five companions (khichdi ke panch yaar): ghee, papad, chutney, dahi and achaar.

I remember once when I got a stomach upset in Imphal, I asked my roommate, a Naga evangelist, to make me some khichdi. She wanted to know the recipe and I told her just to boil some rice and moong dal and fry a little cumin in ghee and pour it over. When she served her khichdi to me, I found small pieces of pork! She felt it would give me strength since I had become weak.

~

I do not remember going out for a meal during my childhood except for an occasional visit to Moti Mahal. It was there that I heard of a dish called butter chicken.

Butter chicken was in fact an invention of Kundan Lal Gujral, a Punjabi refugee from Lahore who came to India during the Partition. In his new home in Delhi, Gujral founded the famous restaurant Moti Mahal, in Daryaganj. The lack of refrigeration apparently led Gujral to put unsold tandoori tikkas into a rich tomato gravy full of butter and cream and the butter chicken was born.

I remember Papa driving us to Moti Mahal. Once, he dropped us outside the restaurant, Amma and I got down from the car and he drove off to park it—without realizing that Amma had fallen into a manhole as she stepped out of the car. She was rescued by passersby and we all had a laugh.

The restaurant used to attract Indian and world leaders, including Zakir Hussain, Jawaharlal Nehru, Richard Nixon and

John F. Kennedy. Freedom fighter and independent India's first education minister Maulana Azad reportedly even told the Shah of Iran, Mohammad Reza Pahlavi, that while in India he must make two visits—to the Taj in Agra and Moti Mahal in Delhi. And the Shah followed his advice, adding his name to the renowned patrons of Moti Mahal. More recently, Moti Mahal was visited by none other than star master chef Gordon Ramsay.

Amma was quite happy to go to Moti Mahal but would never have admitted that butter chicken could compare to any dish made in Lucknow. In any case, she never ate butter chicken.

I must have imbibed these prejudices from my mother. Long after I had graduated, I took some friends to dine at Karim's at Jama Masjid. A family was sitting at the table next to us and I heard a child order butter chicken. Without thinking I told them that this was not the place for butter chicken. They should go to a restaurant serving Punjabi food.

I half expected the family to tell me to mind my own business, as indeed they should have, but a young man turned to me and apologized: 'The children do not know.'

The waiter came to me and apologetically explained that they had to put butter chicken on their menu after repeated demands from their Punjabi customers who did not know, nor appreciated, the difference between Old Delhi's Mughlai food and popular Punjabi food.

The last time I went to Moti Mahal with our family members I remember my cousins—Masi's two sons—whispering amongst themselves. They asked permission to go from Moti Mahal to the newly opened disco called The Cellar in Regal Building, Connaught Place. The Cellar was the first discotheque outside the five-star hotels in Delhi and was designed by Rajeev Sethi (b.1949), the outstanding designer. At the time, I was still in school but later I would visit it to have Western food. Once, when I went with friends I had a steak, and when my friends challenged me, I had a second one. After all, I was born in a family of meat-eating Brahmins.

~

Kashmiri Pandits traditionally did not eat pork, beef or even chicken. But fish and eggs were relished. Perhaps the reason why Kashmiri Pandits did not eat pork was in deference to the Muslims, just like the Kashmiri Muslims did not eat beef in consideration of Hindu beliefs.

It seems almost natural that the Kashmiri Brahmin did not eat pork, but in the *Mahabharata*, King Yudhisthira fed ten thousand Brahmins with pork and venison; and in South Indian literature there were sixteen names for the domestic pig.

And yet during the 1991 election campaign in Tamil Nadu, the Congress candidate from Myiladuthurai, Mani Shankar Aiyar, challenged his opponent to a chicken biryani-eating contest to prove he was a meat-eating Brahmin. Food has always featured in Tamil Nadu's bitter Brahmin-non-Brahmin political battles from the time Brahmin members of the Congress party refused to eat with non-Brahmins.

Although Kashmiri Pandits are traditionally meat-eaters, there are many men and women who are vegetarians. Both my Masi—my mother's older sister—and my Chacha—Papa's younger brother—were strict vegetarians. But neither of them ever objected to anyone in the family eating meat, and in both their homes meat was cooked and relished by other family members.

But in recent times this tolerant attitude is all but gone. A very different kind of vegetarianism is creeping into the culture of the Kashmiris—those who had to leave their homes in the Valley in the aftermath of the insurgency in 1989, and even the downstairs

Kashmiris like my family. I was shocked when I invited an aunt to my home and she told me on the phone: 'Don't order food from the Muslim place in JNU; we can have vegetarian food.' I knew my Mamu, who was also visiting, liked the food from Mughal Darbar, a popular restaurant inside Jawaharlal Nehru University. The kebab-roti reminded Mamu and me of the delicious kebabs with rumali roti and biryani that Nana used to bring for us from the Gymkhana Club in Lucknow. Besides, Kashmiri Pandits always bought halal meat from Muslim butchers. My aunt's intolerance is a reflection of the present times; an intolerance based on the false belief that upper-caste Hindus did not eat meat in the past. But every historian has stated that our ancestors were predominantly non-vegetarian. Not only did my aunt not want to eat food cooked by Muslim hands, she also wanted to impose her distorted, bigoted ideas on us.

~

As I grow older, I sometimes long to taste our traditional Kashmiri food. Sometimes the longing is almost painful. It is not only the food, but also the smells from the kitchen that I long for; something familiar that will remind me of those days when we gathered together as a family. But then the family has drifted apart—I meet them once a year, if that. I think it was the food that bound us together and now the food has disappeared. Kashmiri men no longer know how to cook, and many of them have married women from non-Kashmiri communities who do not enjoy cooking or eating Kashmiri food.

It is virtually impossible to get Kashmiri food unless you know someone who can cook it for you. Even if you are the Prime Minister of India, you will find it difficult to get authentic Kashmiri dum aloo or koftas. In my diary I have recorded an incident which is relevant here. In 1967 Papa was appointed Secretary to Prime Minister Indira Gandhi. Two years later, the government of India decided to nationalize all banks, a move that Papa advocated in consonance with his socialist views. During one of the meetings to finalize the nationalization, Indira Gandhi, in the middle of the discussions, passed a note to Papa. It said, '*Suna hai ki aapka cook bahut acche kofte banata hai. Maine bahut dinon se kofte nahin khaye.*' (I've heard that your cook makes very good koftas. I haven't eaten koftas for a long time). Papa came back home tired and started making koftas for his boss. Amma said, 'Why didn't you tell her we don't have a cook who makes Kashmiri food?' But that was not Papa's style. He could not forget that Indira Gandhi was Jawharalal Nehru's daughter.

The Nehrus like the Haksars belonged to the downstairs Kashmiri Pandit community, and the two families appear to have known each other well. Jawaharlal Nehru was married in one of the Haksar mansions, an event about which I have only read in the papers:

> Sarup Narain ki Haveli, as it was known during the early 19th century, was originally a three-storeyed grandiose structure located at the end of Sadak Prem Narain Bazaar—the intersection of Churiwalan and Bazaar Sita Ram. It was the abode of one of the locality's distinguished Kashmiri pandit families.
>
> "The residence of the Haskars once served as the venue for one of the city's most high-profile weddings in 1916. The relatives and family members of...Jawaharlal Nehru stayed at the mansion when he married Kamala Kaul on February 8. Kamala's family owned another manor called 'Atal House' in the neighbourhood of Bazaar Sita Ram.

Now Jawaharlal and Kamala's daughter was prime minister. She was Indu to Papa's family, how could she be refused? Papa made the koftas and put them in a container and the container was put into a wicker basket. He did not know that Amma had slipped in a hand written note: 'With the compliments of PNH, the chef.'

I remember going to Indira's Gandhi's home sometimes, but she did not serve Kashmiri khana. She must have really been longing for the smells and taste of traditional Kashmiri food to have said in the middle of an important meeting that she wanted to eat koftas!

I no longer meet my family members very often. When we do get together the meals do not give the pleasure we used to get from our traditional cuisine. We have all become very health conscious. No one wants to eat read meat and everyone is on some diet or the other recommended by doctors who warn against eating too much ghee or oil.

Even if there is a traditional wedding and Kashmiri food is served, we have to stand in queue and serve ourselves at the buffet. Buffets do not allow you to sit down and suck out the marrow or chew the bones at leisure. Most times we eat with fork and spoon rather than making luqmas with our hands.

The slow disappearance of our culture and cuisine began long ago, even before we realized what we were losing. By the time my younger sister got married in May 2001, there was only one professional cook who cooked for weddings, Topaji. He, like with many Kashmiri Pandit families, had left his ancestral home in Old Delhi and settled down in Gurgaon. And much of the knowledge of cooking he claimed was from Nandita Bua's book, which was just a home cook's collection of recipes. It can be useful, but I noticed she does not give the recipe for khhatti kaleji.

Some of my aunts and uncles had trained their servants to cook basic Kashmiri food. The most famous was Moti, Dada's cook. But all these men (and they were all men) had disappeared from our lives one by one.

ऊपर की तरह कीमा भून लो जब ३ हिस्से भुन जावे तो गोभी डालकर भून कर पानी डाल दो ताकि गोभी गल जावे लेकिन टुकड़े न हों बीच-बीच में कीमा नीचे से उठा कर फूलों पर डालते रहो इससे गोभी के अन्दर तक क़ीमें का सवाद आ जाता है।

जब खाने को देओ तो फूल हल्के से निकाल कर डिश में रख कर सब क़ीमा कुछ उसके ऊपर चारों तरफ़ डाल हरा धनिया कटा छिड़क कर दो।

आलू कीमा

आलू को छील छोटे-छोटे टुकड़े काट तल लो। क़ीमा जब भुन जाये और गल जाये तो आलू डाल कर दम पर रख दो—इसमें चीनी नहीं पड़ती है।

चने की दाल कीमा

५०० ग्राम चने की दाल को भिगो दो। जब कीमा ३ हिस्से भुन जाये तो दाल डाल कर भूनो। सब मसाला डाल कर एक हाथ चला कर पानी ढाई प्याले डाल दो। दाल गल जावे पर चूरा न होवे। इसमें भी चीनी पड़ेगी। और मटर कीमें की तरह बिल्कुल चिकनाई पर रहेगा।

रौग़न जोश

१ किलो सालन (गोश्त) में

२०० ग्राम घी

१०० ग्राम दही. अदरक बारीक कटी

ढाई चम्मच नमक

दालचीनी के २ टुकड़े, तेज पत्ते;

१ चम्मच लाल मिर्च, ४ लौंग, ४ बड़ी इलायची,

६ छोटी इलायची

डालकर ढकना देकर चढ़ा दो। जब पानी पच जावे सालन लगने लगे तो हींग का पानी डालकर खुरपी से अच्छी तरह खुरच लो। इसी तरह बराबर हींग, और सादा पानी डाल-डाल कर कसुन देओ जब आधा सुर्ख़ हो जावे तो

एक बड़ा चम्मच खसखस भीगी व पिसी

डाल दो और बराबर कसुन देते जाओ जब सुर्ख़ हो जावे तो

१६

A page from Nandita Bua's book of Kashmiri recipes.

In our home, the loss had to do with the disappearance of our meatwala. Every single day, a Muslim meatwala cycled all the way from Jama Masjid to Race Course Road where we lived—a distance of 7 kilometres. Later, we moved to Shanti Niketan in South Delhi, and he now cycled 15 kilometres to our home and then 15 kilometres back. He came on his cycle with a blue wooden box tied to the pillion. It had a net around it, not just to keep away the flies, but also to keep the meat fresh. He announced his coming with a ring of his bicycle bell and Amma would call out to the cook: 'Dekho, meatwala aa gaya.' And then she would have to decide what kind of meat we wanted. Each meat dish had a different cut.

On some days I would stand and watch him cut the meat. Painstakingly, he would remove the fat and the white membranes, and then if we wanted pasandas, he would take each piece and beat it with the back of the knife, or if it was mince, he would mince it in the mincer he carried. It was all done quietly and politely. He never let us down, no matter what the season.

Then one day he told us he was afraid because there were accusations that he and other meatwalas were selling beef. But he still kept coming, till the day he did not turn up. He disappeared from our lives. In those days there were no mobile phones, very few people had phones of any kind, for that matter, and certainly not people of modest means, like our meatwala. And we did not know where he lived. We did not even know his name; at least I do not remember ever calling him by name.

And it was from then on that our cuisine was diminished—we never had pasandas. Now I realize how much more we lost.

2

GROWING UP INDIAN

Amma loved what is today called street food. She loved the chaat and rabri in Lucknow's Chowk; the puris and tea sold on railway platforms. She took me to Old Delhi's Parathewali Gali to have triangular parathas stuffed with grated radish, and to Juhu Beach to slurp sweet golas—ice balls with different coloured syrups poured over them.

Relatives warned Amma that I could get an infection—after all, I was born in London, and returned to India only when I was two. There were relatives who advised making those foods at home, and Amma would say that it is the germs that make outside food so much tastier. If anyone persisted, she would silence them with: 'She will develop immunity to all the germs. Don't worry, she's my daughter, she's tough!'

Amma would have been surprised to know about the role of the bacteria in our guts in keeping good health; that a gram of faeces contains more bacteria than there are people on this Earth. She would have been shocked to learn that in the West people have become so 'clean' that sometimes they need faecal microbiota transplants or stool transplants through colonoscopy, endoscopy or enemas, to get their immune system back in order.

Amma did not need to have all this scientific evidence to back her theory of immunity. Besides, her argument for taking her daughter out to eat street food was a political one. Amma's logic was: 'She is an Indian girl and she must get used to this food.'

~

In 1958-59, when I was barely five years old, my parents decided to go on a road trip all around India. We set off in Papa's maroon-coloured Mercedes from Delhi and went all the way to Kanyakumari, which the British had called Cape Comorin. All my memories of the trip are related to food; it was also my first exposure to the different cuisines of India.

My parents did not plan their journey; they did not book hotels and there were no road maps. In fact, there were no roads in many places. I remember at one point people lifting the heavy car and putting it onto a rickety ferry. Papa drove and we stopped mostly at the homes of our relatives or stayed with his friends.

We motored to Porbander in Gujarat where Chacha was posted. Chacha, as I have said before, was a strict vegetarian, but it would not occur to him not to serve meat to his elder brother's family who had come from so far away.

Both Chacha and Chachi were excited to have us but they were visibly upset that they could not cook any non-vegetarian dish for us. Chachi, who was a non-vegetarian, said the Gujarati neighbours did not allow them even to eat eggs and she had to smuggle them into the house and dispose of the eggshells secretly. This kind of vegetarianism was in contrast to Chacha's vegetarianism, which was so humane.

In Bombay, we stopped at the home of Haru and Jyoti Trevedi, both Gujaratis. Their home was facing the famous Juhu Beach and it was the first time I lived so close to the sea. Amma was thrilled to have ice golas, and I tasted sweet coconut water for the first time in my life. I preferred to drink it straight from the coconut rather than the way Jyoti Masi served it—in a glass. The fun was in drinking from the coconut shell!

Papa announced that we would be visiting the famous Tirupati temple. It was a long drive. Before checking into the guesthouse within the temple compound, my parents instructed me not to ask for meat. When the kind waiter asked what I wanted to eat, I said: 'Fish.' My parents said I did not know what I was talking about. Indignantly I said: 'Machchhali.'

This was the only time in my life when my mother ever told me to lie. If anyone in the temple asked, I was to say that we did not eat meat. It was my first encounter with the bigotry of a certain kind of vegetarianism; it became associated in my young, impressionable mind with intolerance.

We were taken to the sanctum sanctorum in the temple. Papa took off his kurta, since stitched clothes are not allowed. The head priest must have noticed that Papa did not wear the sacred thread. However, Papa spoke to him in chaste Sanskrit, which appeared to make up for the lack of the sacred thread. It was the only time in my life that I had seen anyone conversing in Sanskrit! The temple priest must have wondered what kind of Brahmins we were. He would have been truly shocked if he had known we were meat-eating Brahmins!

In Kerala, we stayed with the family of K.T. Chandy. Uncle KT and Papa had shared an apartment in London while they were students and Papa had done all the cooking while Uncle KT had done the washing up and cleaning. This was my first acquaintance with Syrian Christian cuisine and I loved it; especially the appams and fish or chicken stew cooked in coconut milk.

It was during this time that my sister was born—in September 1959. She already had a tooth and everyone joked that she was ready to chew meat! Apart from the curly-haired baby with a winning smile, I remember tasting red-coloured jelly at the nursing home. Dadi loved jelly, till we told her it was made with hooves of cows. But she never expressed any objection to my enjoying the jelly.

~

Papa always emphasized that a big part of being Indian was to appreciate other people's culture and food while being proud of our own. It also meant learning to enjoy the cuisines of the world because that would be a way for India to be a part of the international community. One of the first books Papa gave me was called *Fun Around the World* by Frances W. Keene, published in New York in 1955. He bought it at the United Nations.

The front page explains the purpose of the book: 'Brief Stories about Boys and Girls of the Countries in the United Nations tell How the Children Live, with the emphasis on How they Play. As Children everywhere understand the Language of Play, this Book introduces the World's Children to Each Other. With each Nation is an Activity related to or derived from that Country.' The book had been written with the 'extensive assistance received from the Delegations to the United Nations.'

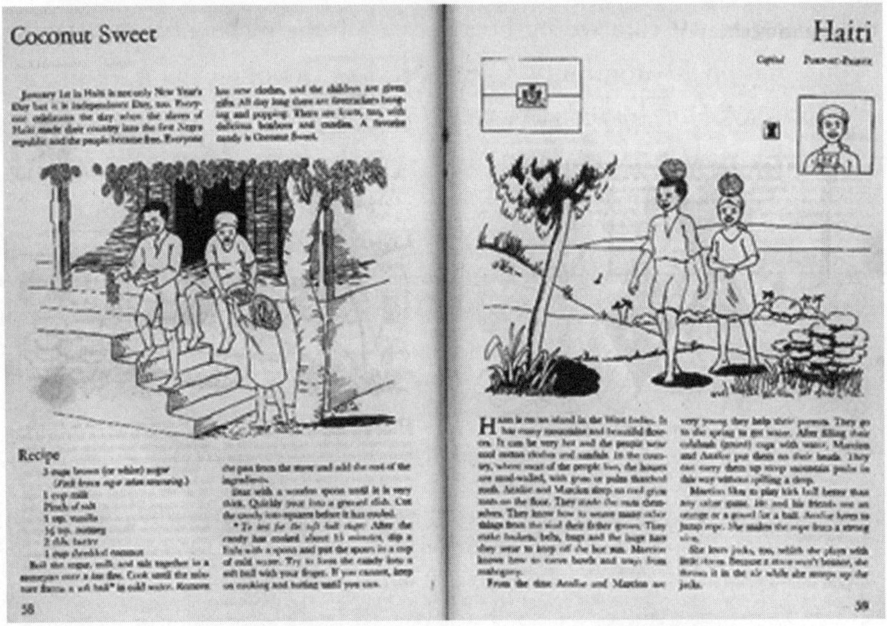

It is from this book I learnt about Haiti being the first country made by slaves. It was such an exciting history. This is how the book introduced Haiti:

> January 1st in Haiti is not only New Year's Day but it is Independence Day, too. Everyone celebrates the day when the slaves of Haiti made their country into the first Negro republic

> and the people became free. Everyone has new clothes, and the children are given gifts. All day long there are firecrackers banging and popping. There are feasts, too, with delicious bonbons and candies.

And I learnt that one of the favourite sweets in Haiti was made with coconut and seemed to be rather like the laddoos Dadi made with sesame seeds or besun, depending on the season and occasion.

Here is the recipe from my yellowed and brittle copy of Fun Around the World:

COCONUT SWEET

Ingredients

- 3 cups of brown (or white) sugar (pack brown sugar when measuring)
- 1 cup of milk
- Pinch of salt
- 1 tsp of vanilla
- ½ tsp nutmeg
- 2 tbsp butter
- 1 cup shredded coconut

Method

- Boil the sugar, milk and salt together in a saucepan over a low fire. Cook until the mixture forms a soft ball in cold water. Remove from the stove and add the rest of the ingredients.
- Beat with a wooden spoon until it is very thick. Quickly pour into a greased dish. Cut the candy into squares before it is cooled.
- To test for the soft ball stage: After the candy has cooked about 15 minutes, scoop out a little with a spoon and put

the spoon in a cup of cold water. Try to form the candy into a soft ball with your fingers. If you cannot, keep on cooking and tasting till you can.

~

In 1960 Papa was posted to Lagos, the capital of newly independent Nigeria. He was going to be India's first High Commissioner and we were going to Lagos by ship!

We boarded the ship in Bombay. Amma and Papa had one cabin and I had a smaller cabin which I shared with Asha Rani, my ayah. There are few memories of the journey: one was the way we threw down coins from the ship and little boys dived down to get them. I do not know where this happened.

The second was my first encounter with white supremacy. At night, everyone had to dress up for dinner and go to the dining room to sit down for a formal meal. I found the formality intimidating. On top of that, the woman next to my cabin shouted at me—I have no memory of why. But I was so scared that I wet my bed every night; something I had never done when I was an infant.

We changed ships at Liverpool and I think it was a ship run by Elder Dempster Company. This was a much friendlier vessel and as we approached Lagos, Papa asked me to look out for a Sikh gentleman who would be there to receive us. That was Gurbachan Singh, the First Secretary.

Uncle Gurbachan, like Papa, had been chosen personally by Prime Minister Jawaharlal Nehru to join the newly created Indian Foreign Service, which was launched vide a cabinet decision of 9 October 1946, with regular recruitment starting in 1948. Prime Minister Nehru chose not only to be his own Foreign Minister, but also took a deep personal interest in the selection and grooming of the personnel for this brand new service to conduct diplomacy and promote the national interests of India in the international arena.

Papa and Amma thought food was an important instrument in forging diplomatic ties and cementing friendships, and with this in mind, decided to organize a Diwali Mela in Lagos. They drew support from the local Indians, one of whom was a young architect whom I remember as Raja Bhai. He made a huge reproduction of the Sanchi Gate as an entrance to the mela. The local Indians, mainly Gujarati and Sindhi, set up food stalls and Uncle Gurbachan put up a magic show.

In Nigeria we had a proper chef, Joseph Gomez. He made hundreds of gulab jamuns from milk powder which were very popular at the mela. The Nigerians enjoyed the spectacle and the novelty of it all and, I am sure, the food.

Joseph Gomez was a Mog. The Mogs are originally from Arakan in Myanmar and belong to a community who ruled over Tripura in the sixteenth century. According to the 2010 census, there were around 32,000 Mogs in Tripura. Mogs were known as cooks and they had evolved their own cuisine. And like our Joseph, they were all self-taught. Joseph was with us till Papa was posted to London in 1966; when we were returning home Joseph said he would stay on and try and open his own restaurant. We lost touch with him.

~

Amma encouraged me to learn some skills from Joseph. Like every artist, he was temperamental and he did not like being disturbed when he was at work. Joseph was rather like a Shaolin master. He said I must first learn to boil an egg in a way that the peel just slips off. I was a bit disappointed that he thought I was not capable of anything more complex. Anyway, I did not have the patience to keep boiling eggs and shelling them.

I remember two desserts that he crafted like works of art. One of them was a huge corn-on-the-cob made with marzipan. I clearly remember the pride with which Joseph would carry in this enormous confection. It looked so real with the green, leafy husk, the silk and the neat rows of kernels on the cob. It looked just like freshly picked maize from a field, except that it had been made with almond marzipan. One real corn on the cob has 16 rows of 800 kernels; and Joseph matched the number with his handmade marzipan.

The other dessert was a basket woven with caramelized sugar served full of fruits and cream. Each guest received one basket. I am sure many of our Nigerian guests still remember those baskets. I do.

I was absolutely delighted to find the recipe in a thin little book called *100 Traditional Recipes from Bengal* by Kamalini Kumar and Sunanada Ray, published by Vikas in 1983 and reprinted in 1992. It has been my constant companion. The last section has a selection of Mog recipes, including cauliflower cutlets, brinjal boats, kedgeree, mutton glace, Bengal jellies, and it includes the Caramel Basket.

CARAMEL BASKET

Ingredients

- 3 tbsp sugar
- 4 kinds of seasonal fruits, diced (e.g. 2 each of bananas,
- peaches, apples and pears)
- 2 teacups of cream (whipped)
- 2 tsps finely powdered sugar
- A little butter
- 1 tsp of brandy

Method

- Grease well with butter a large mould on the inside and put a smaller mould which fits into the larger, on the outside. Put the sugar and 2 tbsp water into a saucepan. Stir over very low heat till the sugar grains dissolve. Simmer without stirring until the mixture turns brown. Be very careful that it does not turn black and gets burnt. Test by putting in a spoon and lifting it up, two threads should appear. Remove from fire
- Pour the mixture immediately into the greased large mould and immediately press the small mould (greased on the outside) into it. Place a weight inside.
- With the remaining caramelized sugar twist handle shapes (optional).
- When cool and set, remove weight and smaller mould. Whip the chilled cream with powdered sugar and brandy. Mix with the diced fruits. Pour the cream and fruits into the sugar basket. Wedge a handle into the basket (optional). The basket will look like brown glass. A conversation point when it is broken and eaten!

~

It was in Nigeria that I saw and tasted a turkey for the first time. Many Nigerians presented Papa with live turkeys. It was also the first time I had a pet, even though it was only for a few days. So when Joseph killed my pet and cooked it, I was distraught and refused to eat it. Amma would not tolerate hypocrisy. She said if I could eat meat, I must learn to kill the animal or bird, otherwise it was hypocrisy. Fortunately, she did not carry this out to its logical end and make me slaughter a goat or a chicken.

My father was a little gentler about my not eating my first pet. But he did not tell me that he, too, had a similar fear of killing animals. I found this out after his death, when I read his autobiography in which he describes how the horror of dissecting a frog put him off biology; he took up mathematics instead. He describes his conversation with the mathematics teacher, Kazi Khurshid Ahmed:

> I turned up at the door of Kazi Khurshid Ahmed, which was open. At first I only saw his back as he was looking out of the window which was opposite the entrance door. My footsteps made him turn around. He was tall, had a beard, but not a flowing one. When he spoke I detected a slight stammer which added passion to his words. I told him the story. At first he laughed but not derisively. He asked me if I was vegetarian. I said no. 'So, you can eat meat, but cannot kill a goat.' I really had no answer to give. All I could say in my defence was that though I ate meat and fish, I could not possibly kill, nor eat the flesh which I associated with a living being I had seen. He did not cross-examine me further.[12]

Reading Papa's account, I realized how much of his daughter I was.

~

The Mizos have a story which reflects the omnivore's dilemma. Their tale is of a time when animals could speak. That made it very difficult to kill them because the animals would plead and cry out for mercy. So the Mizos prayed and, in answer to their prayers, god took away the power of speech from animals and made it easier for them to kill the animals for food.

For the record, I did finally eat my pet turkey cooked by Joseph, but to this day I have not been able to kill an animal...and I still debate with myself on the merits of becoming a vegetarian. The movement for animal rights has become stronger and experts have argued:

> That animal liberation is the logical next step in the forward march of moral progress is no longer the fringe idea it was back in 1975. A growing and increasingly influential movement of philosophers, ethicists, law professors and activists are convinced that the great moral struggle of our time will be for the rights of animals. So far the movement has scored some of its biggest victories in Europe. Earlier this year, Germany became the first nation to grant animals a constitutional right: the words 'and animals' were added to a provision obliging the state to respect and protect the dignity of human beings. The farming of animals for fur was recently banned in England. In several European nations, sows may no longer be confined to crates nor laying hens to 'battery cages'—stacked wired cages so small the birds cannot stretch their wings. The Swiss are amending their laws to change the status of animals from 'things' to 'beings'.[14]

Raising animals for consumption may even become a thing of the past with scientists creating hamburgers from cultured meat. Cultured meat is produced using many of the same tissue engineering techniques traditionally used in regenerative medicine. The first cultured beef burger patty, created by Dr Mark Post at Maastricht University, was eaten at a demonstration for the press in London in August 2013.

The last fifty years have seen a doubling of meat consumption by humans. A 2012 United Nations report estimated that by 2050, meat production would have to increase to 455 million tonnes each year, up from 259 tonnes, in order to satisfy the additional demand generated by population and income growth.

Ngachen Francis, our long-time friend and a plant pathologist and head of the Indian Council of Agricultural Sciences (North East), told us that cattle account for most of our environmental problems, including 19 percent of the world's greenhouse emissions. Meat and dairy products also account for 70 percent of global water consumption and 38 percent of land use. All these reasons have pushed scientists to make meat in their labs and the prospect of the commercialization of this meat, chicken and fish is not too far away. Activists are debating on the long-term effects of these developments.

But in our country, the animal rights movement has been hijacked by the Hindu extremists for a totally different agenda. The militant vegetarianism of the upper-caste Hindutva followers is a far cry from the vegan movement in the West. The vegans strive to avoid animal products in all aspects of their lives, including clothing, cosmetic products, household items and, of course, food. The vegans do not form vigilante groups and beat or kill to enforce their non-violent ideology.

~

There was great deal of excitement in our family when Amma was invited by a television channel in Lagos to give a lesson in Indian cuisine. This was a way of forging the friendship between India and Nigeria, long before we had heard of celebrity chefs. It was very exciting to watch Amma teach her television audience how to make cheese balls.

Amma used cheese, not paneer. They turned out perfectly round and they had a melt-in-the-mouth quality that I remember so often. Unfortunately, I do not have the recipe.

After Nigeria, Papa was posted as Ambassador to Austria in 1964. He was succeeded by P.L. Bhandari, who had a very different idea of diplomacy. In his book entitled *How Not to be a Diplomat*, Mr Bhandari writes: 'Now, I am no angel myself, and I confess that I have always preferred a European or North American posting to any other.' He says he was 'greatly upset' when he was told he was being posted to Nigeria.

Papa, on the other hand, was not terribly excited at the idea of a posting to Vienna because it was not as challenging as a posting to the Third World. But the Indian Embassy was in a beautiful house and it was there that Amma taught me the mystery of how to deal with forks, knives and spoons. She also taught me which glass is used for which alcohol.

My parents insisted on my learning about the local culture and cuisine. Although I was very young, Amma thought it was very important that I be taken to the opera, even though the tickets must have been rather expensive. She said even if I did not understand very much, it would broaden my understanding. She was right—to this day I love the opera.

With Anamika, Amma and Papa in Vienna.

Amma taught me to distinguish between Gothic and Baroque and of course we all appreciated Austrian cuisine. The steaming hot chocolate with whipped cream, the sachertorte or rich chocolate cake with apricot filling, and the apple strudel tasted divine. And then there was the famous Wiener Schnitzel, a thin breaded pan-fried cutlet made from veal. It is considered the national dish of Austria even though it came originally from Italy in 1857. This was the first time I had heard of a 'national' dish.

Papa and I enjoyed beef steaks, and we liked them medium-rare. Amma did not like 'raw meat', as she called them! In Delhi, we did not eat beef because Dadi stayed with us and it would have hurt her sentiments; but more importantly, the servants would not have cooked it.

In Vienna, I witnessed another kind of food diplomacy. Papa had a big reception for the Austrians and the chief guest was none other than the socialist leader Bruno Kreisky (1911–1990), who was at that time Foreign Minister. He would later become Chancellor (1970–1983), and during his time in office he initiated reform in family law, decriminalized abortion and homosexuality, carried out prison reforms and extended benefits to workers, including full sick pay.

There is a black-and-white photograph of my five-year-old sister with two long plaits, dressed in the traditional Austrian dirndl, holding a big platter with cocktail sausages and serving it to Bruno Kreisky who is bent double to pick a sausage from her tray.

I do not remember whether it was after this particular reception or some other party in our house, but one of the guests did not have transport to go back home. Perhaps it was someone from the Embassy. Before Papa could arrange any transport, one of the waiters who had been hired for the occasion offered to drop the guest home in his car. The guest accepted the offer. Later, Amma remarked that she could not believe that people from the working class could afford cars. In the 1960s in India, very few working-class people could afford even a cycle.

In India, the servants would never sit at the same table and have a meal. This was not because my parents had any objection but the servants themselves would have been too embarrassed. In London, my sister and I had our supper with our maid, Lily Miller.

Lily had been in London in 1954 when I was born, and she came back when Papa was posted there again in 1965, when my sister was barely six years old. In the intervening years, whenever Papa passed through London he would inform Lily and our chauffeur, Charlie Hallet. I used to write to both of them and send them Christmas cards.

When I went to London for training as a journalist in 1974, I called on Lily. She invited me to her home in Golders Green. It was such a memorable evening, with tea and hot scones with plenty of butter. She lived there with her younger sister who was eighty years old; Lily was eighty-two and their baby brother, Johnny, was there too. He was just seventy-eight!

~

So I grew up thinking that the sharing of food was a way of forging alliances and making friends across communities and nations. Everywhere we went, I saw how Amma and Papa used food as an instrument to build friendships.

In my diary I have recorded an incident which illustrates how seriously Papa took food as a tool of diplomacy. It was around the time of the signing of the Indo-Soviet Friendship Treaty of 1971 in the wake of the Indo-Pak war; the Russians had supported India, while the USA and China had supported Pakistan. Papa suggested that the Russian delegates be served cold soup, which was an important part of Soviet cuisine. But Indira Gandhi insisted on hot soup. Papa disagreed. The Prime Minister then decided to ask D.P. Dhar, India's Ambassador to the Soviet Union. D.P. Dhar was a bit worried when he was called away from a banquet at the Rashtrpati Bhavan to attend a call from the PM. He must have wondered why on earth the PM was asking him, 'Do Russians prefer hot soup or cold soup?' He replied without much thought. 'Hot soup.' Indira Gandhi looked triumphantly at Papa. Later, D.P. Dhar found out that he had let down his friend and apologized to Papa.

Amma and Papa made sure we learnt to appreciate the food and lifestyle of different cultures, while having pride in our own culture and cuisines. This may all sound naive, but those were different times. It was around that time, in November 1966, that the General Conference of the United Nations Educational, Scientific and Cultural Organization (UNESCO) passed the Declaration of the Principles of International Cultural Co-operation. Article One reads:

1. Each culture has a dignity and value which must be respected and preserved.
2. Every people have the right and the duty to develop their culture.
3. In their rich variety and diversity and in reciprocal influences they exert on one another, all cultures form a part of the common heritage belonging to all mankind.

~

When I think of the Wiener Schnitzel, I cannot help speculating whether we in India could ever decide upon a national dish. With all the noise about one language, one nation, one culture, what about a national dish?

There is speculation in the media that the humble khichdi may be declared as the national dish of India. As the first step, celebrity chef Sanjeev Kapoor and celebrity yoga instructor and businessman Baba Ramdev cooked 918 kgs of the dish. The tadka, or seasoning, alone consumed 25 kgs of ghee, 1 kg of turmeric powder and 500 grams of cumin seeds! The feat has been entered in the Guinness Book of Records, and the khichdi was distributed among the poor.

If we must have a national dish (although I don't understand the need for one), khichdi would be good choice: after all, nearly every state has its own version, from the bisi bele huli anna of Karnataka, to the pongal of Tamil Nadu, to the keeme ki khichdi of Hyderabad, to the simple moong dal khichdi, which many of us have when we have a stomach upset.

Foreign travellers to India over the centuries noticed the dish and the Mughals—Aurangzeb, Akbar and Jehangir—all loved their khichdi. Michelin-starred chefs have invented their own versions, such as the black olive khichdi, the lobster khichdi, and some versions have fifty different ingredients.

The declaration of khichdi as a national dish should be welcomed; but will the government try and arrive at one national recipe? That is when the controversies will start.

There have already been bitter controversies over declaring tea as a national drink. Punjab wanted the national drink to be milk, whereas the coffee growers claimed that it should be coffee.

The most serious conflict regarding a food item was over the 'nationality' of the rosgulla. I had been brought up to believe it was quintessentially Bengali. Once, at a seminar in 2011, in Dibrugarh, I remarked: 'Whatever we may think of the Bengalis (I was referring to the Assam–Bengal differences), their sweets are out of this world.' My remark was made in a lighter vein; however, it provoked an angry response from Pratibha Ray, a Sahitya Akademi winner from Odisha. She said it was not a Bengali invention but originally from Odisha.

I remembered Pratibha Ray's remarks when, a few years later, a war broke out between West Bengal and Odisha over the origins of the rosgulla. It started in September 2015, when the Directorate of Food Processing Industry of West Bengal sent in an application (number 533) seeking the GI (geographical indication) status for Banglar Rasogolla. According to the World Intellectual Property Organization: 'A geographical indication is a sign used on products that have a specific geographical origin and possess qualities or a reputation that are due to that origin.' Essentially, the GI tag provides an assurance of quality and uniqueness, which are attributable to the place of a product's origin. The tag ensures that the product gets a premium pricing in domestic and international markets.

Odisha claimed that the rosgulla's origins were in the temples of Odisha and set up a committee to investigate into the matter. The committee was headed by eminent Jagannath cult scholar Asit Mohanty, and it submitted a 100-page report. In support of Odisha's claim, the committee had pointed to the sweet's reference in the Dandi Ramayana, a version of the epic adapted by Balaram Das in the sixteenth century. The report also claimed that the sweet had been offered to gods in mutts and temples for over six hundred years.

According to the legendary historian of Indian food, Kollegal Thammu (K.T.) Achaya, the splitting of milk was a taboo in India (so it could not have been offered to the gods) till the Portuguese introduced cottage cheese, which was the origin of the chhana-based sweets in Bengal, in contrast to the khoya-based sweets in other parts of the country.[12] Before the introduction of cottage cheese, rosgullas could only have been made by splitting milk.

After due procedure (examination, objections, hearing, opposition and appeal), the GI tag was finally conferred on Bengal in July 2017. Bengal has already got the GI tags for many of its sweets, including Joynagarer Moa, Bardhman Sitabhog and Bardhman Mihidana.

Odisha has not entirely lost the battle. The GI tag has been given only for Banglar Rasogolla; Odisha has applied for a GI tag for its Pahala rosgulla. Pahala is a village between Bhubaneshwar and Cuttack where you can get the best of Odisha's sweets from its fifty or more sweet shops on either side of the highway. I have learnt much about the delicious world of Odisha sweets, such as Chenna Poda which is like a baked cheesecake. Just for the record, I learnt about Chenna Poda from a law student of mine; she is a Bengali!

~

I have learnt that as far as cuisines are concerned, one must be very careful in conversation. My parents had made me aware of regional differences, but I discovered that the intra-regional divisions were as important for our people. I remember once I proudly announced to a Bengali friend that I could make bhapa doi, a Bengali dessert made by steaming yoghurt. Amma had learnt it from her Bengali friend, Deepali Nag (1922–2009). Amma's friendship with Deepali went back to their childhood when Amma's father was posted in Agra and Deepali was learning classical music from the famous Faiyaz Khan of the Agra Gharana.

Amma told me that in those days it was rare for educated women from upper-class families to learn music, so Deepali was a pioneer.

It was in Deepali's home that Amma got a taste of Bengali food and learnt some dishes which became a part of the food cooked in our home. And bhapa doi was one of my favourites. We thought nothing about including Bengali dishes or for that matter any other cuisine into our everyday meals—that was an integral part of being Indian.

So when I mentioned bhapa doi to this Bengali friend, I was not prepared for his answer: 'Bhapa doi is from West Bengal.' 'West' was said with contempt. He said his parents were originally from East Bengal, which is the home of real Bengali cuisine.

I had almost forgotten all about bhapa doi till I tasted it again in Imphal's Classic Hotel. It brought back so many memories that when we went back home to Goa I tried my hand at making the dessert again; but being too lazy to steam it, I baked it. And I used one of Amma's shortcuts: condensed milk. It turned out delicious.

The last time I saw Deepali Nag was at my mother's funeral where she sang a special song in her memory.

Controversies over food are as sharp within each state as they are between states. They reflect the deep divisions within our society. Even a small state like Kerala has five distinct cuisines: the ancient community of Syrian Christians; the Muslims or the Moplahs who are the descendants of Arab traders who married Kerala women; the Thiyas, the community which formerly tapped toddy; the Nairs, the original warrior caste; and the Namboothiris, who are a community of Brahmins.

The tiny state of Goa also has five cuisines according to Odette Mascarenhas, who has written a book on the culinary heritage of the state: Saraswat, Hindu Goan, Muslim Goan, Portuguese Goan and Christian Goan.[13] I have heard the Hindu Goans complain that the Goan Catholics do not know how to make a proper curry because they put cumin in it!

~

In Nigeria I had started reading Enid Blyton (1897–1968) and loved her school stories. What caught my imagination were the midnight feasts by the girls in Malory Towers.

It was largely due to Enid Blyton's descriptions of boarding schools where the girls had midnight feasts with fruit cakes, cream buns, chocolates and improvised lemonade drinks that I agreed to go to a boarding school. In fact, I was positively excited by the idea. My parents' motivation was to ensure I did not grow up far from India; and more importantly, that I learnt Hindi and Indian history.

So I found myself in Welham Girls' High School in Dehra Dun for my ninth birthday. The principal was Grace Mary Linnell (1900–1970). Miss Linnell was extremely tall and thin and had bright blue eyes which seemed to see everything; even deep into the soul of her students. Miss Linnell was keen to bring us up as Indians and a part of this was to instill in each of us a respect for all religions. Our prayers were certainly 'secular'; we prayed for the leaders of the world, animals of the world; the devotional songs we sang were always inspired by the Sufi or Bhakti traditions.

Before joining Welham's, Miss Linnell had taught at the Mahbubia Girls' School in Hyderabad. She was twenty-two years old when she joined that school. She was very careful that the girls followed their own culture and customs. So, she insisted that the Muslim girls in Welham's keep roza during the month of Ramzan and she made provision for sehri and iftar.

The trouble was that in our school we did not have many Muslim girls, and the only one in my class, Rummana Habibullah

(1952–1999), was from a family which was not very religious. Her parents were from Lucknow and knew my parents. Rummana insisted I join her for iftar (I never got up in time for sehri, which was before sunrise). That was the first time I had heard of iftar and I enjoyed the food with Rummana and Jamal, who was our only Muslim waiter. What I liked more than the food was the equality between Jamal, Rummana and myself as we sat at the same table and shared a meal.

Rummana went on to become a well-known painter and a pioneer of conceptual art, installations and political engagement in art. She became known by her married name of Rummana Hussain. I believe the demolition of the Babri Masjid was a turning point in her life as an artist. The last time I spoke to her was just a few months before her death in 1999, when she invited me to Bombay where she was staying, fighting the cancer which was destroying her. I could not go because I, too, was not well.

I did not understand why Miss Linnell insisted on us speaking in Hindi on Tuesdays, which was also the day we had a vegetarian meal of rice, kadi with pakoras and pumpkin. And one Tuesday of the month we had to write to our parents in pure Hindi, normally dictated to us by our Hindi teacher. I still remember the first line of the letter began: *Adarniya Mataji aur Pitaji, saadar pranam* (respected Mother and Father, respectful greetings). When my parents received the letter they were both shocked and amused; especially when I told them that I had not written it on my own.

I loved Miss Linnell; she was good to me. But I was not happy in the boarding school because the other girls had been brought up with very different values, even though we did have a few midnight feasts.

The leaders who organized the feasts managed to get tins of Milkmaid condensed milk and jam by asking the day scholars to smuggle these items in. There were tins of Bournvita which we enjoyed eating, and bread which we saved from breakfast. We sat in the bathroom and enjoyed the goodies, but our midnight feasts were not half as exciting as the ones described in Enid Blyton's books.

I was so unhappy at Welhams that when Papa was posted to the UK in 1966, my parents took me out of boarding school and put me into a school in London.

~

While Papa was Acting High Commissioner in the UK, he was invited to inaugurate a shirt factory owned by an Indian. If I remember correctly the man called himself Mr Paul. He told Papa that he had changed his name from Pal to Paul so he could fit in better.

Papa asked him how he had arrived in England. He said that in his youth he had asked his father why India was so poor and Britain so rich. His father told him that British rule was like a cow—her mouth was in India where we kept her well fed, while her udders were in England so they got all the milk. After hearing this story from his father, Pal decided he would go to England and reverse the mouth of the cow.

Papa was asked to inaugurate a new Indian restaurant in London, called Gaylord. This was in the summer of 1966. It has since been voted as one of the five best Indian restaurants in London. The cuisine is mostly Punjabi, with chicken tikka masala and black dal with plenty of butter. At the time when Papa was invited to inaugurate Gaylord, Indians could not have imagined that chicken tikka masala would one day be declared the UK's national dish. In 2001, the British Foreign Secretary, Robin Cook, gave a speech in which he hailed chicken tikka masala as a symbol of modern multicultural Britain.

While Indians were celebrating that an Indian dish had acquired such an iconic status in Britain, there were counter-claims that the origin of the chicken tikka masala was not Indian—it was either Bangladeshi or Pakistani. The fight over chicken tikka masala was carried out in the media. An Indian food critic, Rahul Verma, who writes for *The Hindu*, said he first tasted the dish in 1971 and that its origins were in the Punjab. He said it was basically a Punjabi dish not more than forty or fifty years old and must have been made accidentally.

Another version of the story is that a Pakistani chef, Ali Ahmed Aslam, proprietor of the Shish Mahal restaurant in the West End of Glasgow, invented chicken tikka masala by improvising a sauce made from yogurt, cream, and spices. In 2013, his son, Asif Ali, told the story of its invention on a BBC cookery programme.

The story goes:

> On a typical dark, wet Glasgow night [in 1971], a bus driver coming off his shift came in and ordered a chicken curry. He sent it back to the waiter saying it's dry. At the time, Dad had an ulcer and was enjoying a plate of tomato soup. So he said why not put some tomato soup into the curry with some spices. They sent it back to the table and the bus driver absolutely loved it. He and his friends came back again and again and we put it on the menu.[14]

The number of Indian restaurants in European and American countries has increased significantly and one in seven curries sold in the UK is chicken tikka masala. But have Indians benefited from this boom? In an ironic inversion of history, British companies now export chicken tikka masala to Pakistan, India and Bangladesh. I wonder what Mr Paul would say to this. Can the cow ever be turned around?

~

In 1970, I joined Delhi University as an undergraduate student. I decided to take up sociology, a subject that had been introduced recently and it was taught at the Delhi School of Economics, which was a post-graduate institute. In the middle of the campus was a branch of India Coffee House. That is where I learnt to appreciate filter coffee and enjoyed idlis and dosa for lunch.

By this time, Papa was back in India and was appointed Secretary to Prime Minister Indira Gandhi. It was sometime then that Papa switched to having coffee on the doctor's advice; I do not remember why the doctor had so advised. But Amma bought freshly ground South Indian coffee every week from the shop run by the India Coffee House.

The food and coffee in India Coffee House was good and very cheap. There was a reason behind this. Coffee had been grown in India by native Indians since the sixteenth century and the concept of coffee houses began to gain a little popularity in the eighteenth century in Chennai (Madras State) and Calcutta. However, the English rulers did not allow Indians to enter these coffee houses, and in reaction to this discrimination, the idea of an 'India Coffee House' was born.

The India Coffee House chain was started by the Coffee Cess Committee in 1936, when the first outlet was opened in Bombay. In the course of the 1940s, there were nearly fifty coffee houses all over British India. However, due to a change in policy in the mid-1950s, the Coffee Board decided to close down the coffee houses. This was what inspired the communist leader A.K. Gopalan to organize the workers of the coffee houses and demand that the coffee houses be handed over to them.

The movement compelled the Board to hand over the outlets to the workers who then formed the Indian Coffee Workers' Co-operatives and renamed the network as Indian Coffee House. A co-operative began in Bangalore on 19 August 1957, and one was established in Delhi on 27 December 1957.

Many years later, a Bangalore-based Naxalite friend told me about a Muslim saint who brought coffee to India. The saint's name was Baba Budan. While returning from a pilgrimage to Mecca, he smuggled seven coffee beans (by tying them around his waist) from Yemen to Mysore. He planted them on the Chandragiri Hills, now named after the saint as Baba Budan Giri (giri means 'hill') in Karnataka's Chikmagalur district.

Systematic cultivation soon followed Baba Budan's first planting of the seeds in 1670, mostly by private native Indian owners, and the first plantation was established in 1840 on Baba Budan Giri and its surrounding hills.

The tomb of Baba Budan attracts thousands of pilgrims, both Hindus and Muslims. The land has belonged to the Waqf Board of Karnataka since 1964 but in 1978 a local Hindu leader claimed that it was Hindu land and filed a petition in support of his claim. After the Hindutva forces demolished the Babri Masjid in Ayodhya in 1992, they became bolder in their bigotry. The first incident of hoisting saffron flags at the tomb of Baba Budan was reported in December 1999 when the Bajrang Dal threatened to storm the shrine in order to 'liberate' it of its Sufi heritage. Many writers and activists protested, but the Hindutva forces have stated that their objective is to turn the Budan Giri range of Chickmagalur into the 'Ayodhya of the South'.

Since my husband Sebastian and I were now living in Goa, we thought it would be a good idea to drive down to see for ourselves the tomb of Baba Budan. We set off in November 2014 in our car. The drive from Goa to Chikmagalur is beautiful. We drove through the coffee plantations to the Thippanahalli Homestay, an old mansion built in 1934, offering accommodations. It is situated on the slope of Baba Budan Giri at an elevation of 4,100 ft with a breathtaking backdrop of Mullaiahnagiri, the tallest peak in Karnataka.

The next day, we drove to Baba Budan's shrine. We arrived in a good mood; the fresh air and the beauty had uplifted our spirits. But one look at the shrine at the bottom of some thirty-to-forty steps made my heart heavy. There were separate entrances for Hindus and Muslims.

One of the two entrances to Baba Budan's shrine—all metal spikes and barbed wire.

I did not identify with either. Sebastian, my husband, is a Christian. There was no entrance for him or for non-believers like me. The Hindutva forces had succeeded in desecrating the oldest Sufi shrine in South India with their hate-filled communal politics. The whole area was guarded by men in uniform carrying guns.

~

In 1971, I witnessed the birth of a new nation, Bangladesh. I was involved in collecting clothes for the refugees who were pouring across our borders, and met Bangladeshi leaders who came to talk to Papa. Many of them had formed a government in exile.

Papa asked whether I would like to go across the border of the new nation. I went with a friend, Gauri Panikkar, and we were taken by car by a Bangladeshi friend. That was when I saw first-hand the horrific conditions of the refugees and the devastation of the villages. I do not remember which village we went to, but the villagers got us fresh fish from their pond and made a most delicious meal. It was not only well cooked, but also served with a great deal of warmth, and the hospitality was overwhelming.

In 1998, when my father died, the Bangladesh High Commissioner came to pay his condolences. He said he had been the District Collector when I had visited Bangladesh. I recounted the story of how we had been given a wonderful meal and how I loved hilsa (*Tenualosa ilisha*). I was really embarrassed (and I have to admit, very pleased) when the next day the chauffeur of the High Commissioner brought an entire hilsa fish—raw and ready to be cooked. I did not dare even joke that I could not possibly cook it as well as the Bangladeshis, just in case they then sent me cooked hilsa!

Hospitality is a core value in South Asia. One of the most heart-rending stories which demonstrates this is from Meghalaya. It tells the story of how the humble betel nut or kwa as they call it, became central to Khasi society. Here is the story:

> Once upon a time, there were two friends. One was very rich and another one was extremely poor. They grew up together and had known each other since childhood.
>
> One day, the rich guy told the poor friend that he wanted to visit his house and meet his family as, since childhood, he had never been to his friend's house.

To which the poor guy invited his rich friend for lunch any time he wanted and promised to serve him food. So the rich guy made a surprise visit to his poor friend's little house. As per his promise, the poor guy went to the kitchen and asked his wife to cook something for his rich friend but unfortunately they didn't have anything to cook. The poor guy went to nearby houses to ask for some rice, but no one offered him anything and he returned empty-handed.

The poor guy felt embarrassed to go in front of his rich friend without any food, so he took a knife and killed himself. Seeing this, the wife also killed herself because nothing was left in this world for her without her husband. The rich guy waited for long and finally decided to go inside the kitchen. When he went, he found two bodies on the ground covered with blood, the water was boiling over the stove and all boxes in the kitchen were empty. He realized his friend had killed himself because they were not able to serve him food. So he took the knife and killed himself too.

A thief came and found three dead bodies. He felt if he went out of the house and anyone found him, they would beat him to death for killing a family, so he also killed himself.

God was looking from heaven and realized four innocent people had died because a poor man was not able to serve anything to his guest. So God decided to gift Meghalaya betel-nut trees.

Now anyone, rich or poor, can serve something to their guest. And from that time, everyone in Meghalaya eats betel nut and welcomes their guest with the same. It is claimed that the poor guy is the leaf and his wife is the betel nut. The rich guy is tobacco and the thief is lime.[15]

~

In 1985 I went for a peace march through Central America. It was in part to protest against the role of the USA. A delegation from our group was invited by the Foreign Ministry and I was included. I was wondering what we would be given to eat. I took for granted that we would be treated to an elaborate tea, but when we went there we were not even offered water.

Recently, Sebastian and I went to Chile and stayed with a Chilean friend we met through couchsurfing. I thought we would be offered a hot meal, but our host did not even offer us a cup of tea. However, we found he had given up his bedroom for us, complete strangers, because it had an attached bathroom.

We South Asians can overwhelm people with our hospitality and sometimes it is really over the top.

~

In college I had two friends: Naina Malse, a Maharashtrian, and Poonam Narain, who belonged to the Mathur community of Old Delhi. (Her father was the first and only person I have known personally who had learnt Esperanto, the international language made from words of several of the world's many languages.) Poonam lived in a big sprawling house in Civil Lines and I was in and out of her home and enjoyed the food there. I was there to share the excitement when Naresh, Poonam's brother, got married and Indu, the new daughter-in-law, came to live in their home. She was a good cook and it was the first time I saw how mayonnaise was made. But what I remember the most are the meat chops made by their khansama—he made big balls of mincemeat held together on a bone. This is one recipe I wish I had written down.

I was also there when Poonam got married. The family was so large and the excitement so great that when the baraat arrived, people realized that the cold drinks were not ready. I rushed to get packets of Rasna powder in different flavours; quickly mixed the drinks in water and had them ready by the time the bridegroom's party walked into the house.

When Poonam's father heard that I had made the Rasna he was angry because I should not have been made to work; as an unmarried girl I was Goddess Lakshmi incarnate!

Remembering this incident, I think it is strange that even in the 1970s people did not serve aerated cold drinks at parties.

Poonam and I having aloo-chaat in Delhi.

The last time I met Poonam was when I suddenly saw her with her family in Goa. It was probably in 1997. Indu and Naresh were buying alcohol for their daughter's wedding. Things had changed dramatically.

~

I did not attend Naina's wedding because by then I was doing journalism in London. But I was present at her sister's wedding and learnt the intricacies of serving guests in a Chitpavan household on that occasion. Those lessons helped me appreciate a typical Chitpavan Brahmin lunch served by my sister-in-law

Ranjana, a proud Maharashtrian, who married my Masi's younger son, Sanat Kaul.

Ranjana and Sanat Kaul's son's wedding was in 2017, and was in part Kashmiri and in part Bihari (since the bride was from Bihar). But Ranjana decided to have a Maharashtrian lunch on the day of his sacred thread ceremony, or the Divgun and Yagnopavitra ceremony.

It was a sit-down lunch and we each had big thalis with katoris in front of us. I found myself sharing the table with Janameyjaya, my two-year-old grandnephew, the grandson of my cousin Arvind and Manmohini Kaul (the same one who had been distressed by the presence of dal at her wedding reception). Next to the little man were his ayah, then his nani, Manmohini, and the most elegantly dressed Arti, exuding imperious dignity. She was Sanat and Arvind's cousin from their father's side of the family.

Arti told Manmohini that she should send Janameyjaya to her to learn traditional etiquette. I could imagine the little boy being taught how to say adaab, perhaps a bit of Urdu poetry and appreciation of the fine art of dining.

I was busy licking the chutneys and raita on my plate and encouraged my grandnephew to do the same, but he did not want to try new things. I pointed out the delicately golden fried kurdaya with thin batter and told him to try the pakora. And he answered: 'Pakore aise nahi hote hain.' To him they did not look like the usual orange-coloured greasy pakoras which he had seen.

That was when I gave him a lecture. I told him that there are many kinds of pakoras, and his Dadi (Ranjana) came from Maharashtra, his father was from U.P. and his Nani was a real Kashmiri from Kashmir. And we all had different kinds of food and we should learn to like all these different kinds of food.

Much to the amazement of the other guests sitting at our table, the little boy picked up the Maharashtian pakora and ate it. His nani remarked: 'I don't know how he is listening to you.' I knew it was Amma's training. And I knew that the etiquette Arti had in mind did not include respect for other people's cuisines, because she had already shown her disapproval of the small portions of food, served course-by-course.

It was not only Arti; the other Kashmiri guests were also amazed at the cuisine. They were not used to being served such small helpings or so many courses. Kashmiris do not have courses; at least, downstairs Kashmiris don't. We like to have a heap of rice and mix tasty luqmas, blending different flavours according to our whim or fancy.

I went back home in Mamu's car. He was forthright as usual: 'When I saw the helpings, I thought we would go back hungry, but I am feeling so full.'

Here is the menu of that day, sent to me by Ranjana after I told her that I wanted to include it in my book (she has marked Janameyjaya's pakoras for me):

MENU

Ishan's Yagnyopavit & Divgun

12th December 2016

Served during puja:

- Tomato saar
- Small kothmbir vadi (hara dhania)
- Small batata bhonda (potato)

Lunch: traditional sit down—served in silver thalis

Accompaniments with main meal
(a guest will find these already served in the thali)

- Salt, nimbu, ghee
- Mango pickle

- Fresh green chuney (hara dhania-coconut- green chilly)
- Kakdi chi Koshimbir (salad: kheera-lemon juice-roasted peanuts-salt/little sugar)
- Lal Bhopla Bharit (lal kaddu–dahi raita)
- Kurdaya-kanda bhajji (Janameyjaya's pakoras!!)
- Papad

Main meal:

Rice:

- Sadha bhat (plain white rice) with varan (arhar dal without masala) and ghee
- Masala bhat

Vegetables:

- Batata Bhaji (boiled potato sukha subji)
- Aloo patal bhaji (arvi patta curry-ish)
- Bharli vangi (bhare baingan)
- Matki usal (sprouted motth dal—you had this yesterday)

Roti:

- Sadhi poli (plain roti)
- Puri

Meetha:

- Puran poli
- Motichur ladu (very small boondi)
- Kheer

Even seventy years after independence we did not know about each other's cuisines, let alone appreciate and celebrate the diversity. When will we ever learn?

I went off to London for a year's training in journalism at the end of 1974 and was attached to the *Times Educational Supplement*, which was then a part of the Times group of publications.

On the day I joined, I sat opposite a colleague whose name was Philip Vennings. He was quite friendly and we introduced ourselves; in the middle of the conversation he went off and returned with a big bar of chocolate. I thought to myself that he would offer me some and I was wondering whether I should accept a piece or just politely refuse. We continued to chat as he tore the wrapper. And then, he bit into the chocolate without any self-consciousness and continued our conversation. I was shocked that he had not offered any to me. And I watched him polish off the entire bar without a trace of embarrassment over eating it by himself, without even formally offering some to his new colleague.

This was the first big cultural shock. More recently, I have met Indian students studying in the USA and they have had similar reactions. They find it difficult not to share their meals with fellow students or to eat alone.

From London I was sent to Blackburn where I advertised in the newspaper: 'Indian journalist wants to stay with British working-class family.' I got a response from Michael, a milkman, and his wife, Carol. I stayed with them and got a glimpse into the life of ordinary English people. The couple were very warm and I felt at home. Carol offered to wash my clothes in her washing machine, but I was not sure what would happen to my six-yard silk sari. She had a solution—she put it into a pillowcase and then washed it and it came out safe and sound. She even darned the holes at the elbows of my cardigan.

We had our evening meal around five, but sometimes I would come later from office and Carol would always make me a warm meal. One day, I came back to find they had gone out and left a note for me to help myself to anything I liked in the fridge.

I have never liked cooking, so I went to bed after having some bread and probably tea. I was fast asleep when loud knocking woke me up. Carol had come back and checked in the fridge and in the kitchen and when she found I had not eaten, she cooked me a toad-in-the-hole and was now waking me up to have a hot meal!

Toad-in-the-hole is sausage cooked in Yorkshire pudding batter. Apparently, the dish appears in print as early as 1762, where it is referred to as a 'vulgar' name for a 'small piece of beef baked in a large pudding'. For me, toad-in-the-hole will forever be associated with the warmth of an English working-class home.

Before leaving London, after a year of working with different papers, I was invited for lunch by Denis Hamilton (1918–1988), to the penthouse. His wife and his secretary were also present. Denis Hamilton (before he was knighted) was then the Chief Executive of Times Newspapers and I was aware of the honour and could not help feeling a little intimidated.

When the lunch arrived, it was the usual English fare: one chicken and two veg, including boiled peas. As I cut the chicken and tried to put the peas on my fork, one pea rolled out of my plate.

I watched the pea; so did everyone else. For an excruciating second I wondered what I should do: try and rescue it or pretend it did not exist? If my rescue op failed, I would look even more ridiculous, so I let the pea be. We continued our lunch without incident.

~

I was back in India towards the end of the Emergency. It was then I learnt how they had arrested Dada and Pupha from Pandit Brothers and tried to frame them in a false income-tax case. This was revenge by Indira Gandhi against Papa for his criticism of the way she was pampering her younger son, Sanjay Gandhi.

That was when I learnt about the strange consequences of accepting presents given in friendship. In March 1962, Jacqueline Kennedy, the First Lady of the USA, came to India on a visit. During her visit she spoke of how each day in India she had 'new experiences, new friends, and new welcomes'. One of these new friends was Gopal Narian, the manager of Pandit Brothers, Dada's shop in Connaught Place.

Jacqueline was going to throw a party and needed a very special tablecloth. She was known for her style and she wanted damask, on rich and heavy silk or linen. She was informed that the only person who could find it for her was Gopalji.

Gopalji told me this story himself. He said he was overwhelmed by the request from the First Lady herself and he used all his contacts to find her damask—a white on white embroidered fabric—for her dining table. She was so pleased, she presented him with a bottle of some very expensive champagne. Gopalji kept the bottle and still had it with him in 1975 when Indira Gandhi declared a national Emergency.

Gopalji had seen how they had dragged Dada and my Bua's husband, K.P. Mushran, who was the general manager of the shop, to the police station and taken their fingerprints; the police had also arrested the manager of Pandit Brothers, Mathur, and he had spent a day in Tihar Jail before being bailed out. Gopalji was afraid that if the tax department raided his home, they could find the famous gift of friendship. Who would believe the diminutive man's story that the precious bottle was a gift from the First Lady of America? Gopalji broke the bottle and poured the contents down the toilet and got rid of the evidence of friendship before it landed him in jail.

~

Amma faced a similar problem. Papa stopped drinking alcohol after I was born, and only took to drinking again when Amma died and he had lost his eyesight. Over the years, he had accumulated many friends from across the globe and diplomats sent him expensive alcohol for Christmas or New Year. There was quite a collection of them in my parents' home in Shanti Niketan.

The bottles were obviously expensive and I know Amma gave them regularly to Nikhil Chakravarty, the editor of *Mainstream Weekly*, to sell and make a bit of money for his publication, which was run on a shoestring budget. It was an act of solidarity with Uncle Nikhil, a friend and comrade. In 1975, there were still a lot of bottles of expensive alcohol in the store room and during the Emergency when Indira Gandhi had targeted Papa for opposing Sanjay Gandhi's projects, there was every possibility of a raid. Amma knew it would be difficult to explain how they had this collection; they had no proof of origin. She knew it was easier to prove a guilty man innocent than to prove one's own innocence.

That is when Amma, too, took all those tokens of international friendship (I do not know how many) and poured their contents into the toilet!

~

It took some months before the case was finally settled and Pandit Brothers won with its integrity in check. Amma wrote a small book on the whole incident called *That Case of Pandit Brothers* (1978), which was published by Nikhil Chakravarty.

~

By the 1980s all our elders had passed away, and so when my younger sister decided to get married in 2001, my husband and I were the elders who had to take responsibility for the wedding arrangements. My sister's fiance's family was also from Old Delhi, but from a business community. It was a very different Delhi culture from ours, as we soon found out.

It was on 29 April 2001 that we set out from our home in Shanti Niketan for Ravindra's home in the by-lanes of Old Delhi. We were carrying baskets of fruits and sweets for the bridegroom and presents for the family.

The most difficult decision I had to make was about the mithai to be taken to the bridegroom's home. Traditionally, we had always bought mithai from Old Delhi and it was probably from Ghantewale ki Dukaan. But the groom's family lived in the heart of Old Delhi and they would know the best places. What mithai could I take which would match them in richness, textures and sheer variety?

Being brought up as Indians, I thought we should not be bound by such traditions. Besides, in our home, everyone preferred Bengali sweets, which were made with chhana or paneer rather than the rich khoya. So I decided to take Bengali mithai from Annapoorna. It was a way of asserting our pan-Indian identity.

I do not remember how many boxes of mithai I bought, but it was an odd number since odd numbers are considered auspicious. And I bought as many different kinds as possible: kheer kadams, labang latikas, sandesh of many shapes and sizes and a few sticky sweets which would not drip in case the boxes leaked.

We must have seemed quite a strange party: me, my Naga husband, my sister's friend Achala in a sari and our driver. In single file we walked the length of the narrow lane and climbed up to the house. We sat with the boxes of sweets, fruits and saris. There was silence.

Ravindra's parents, too, were no more, and his father's sister, the Bua, was officiating as the elder. It was Bua who first broke the silence and asked what we would be cooking for the wedding day. They were relieved that we would not have non-vegetarian dishes on the day the puja was to be performed.

Bua asked what the typical Kashmiri dishes were. I have no idea why but I mentioned the one I think is the tastiest—khatte begun or brinjals cooked with tangy tomatoes, of course without onions. Sebastian loved the way Chacha had cooked it for him.

Bua was shocked: 'But we never serve brinjals at any auspicious occasion.' Now, what would be a diplomatic answer? Should we not have brinjals cooked and replace them with something else? I decided that we should each stick to our own cuisines…

When we returned it was with many boxes of sweets. The moment we got back we opened them. All of them had Karachi halwa. Every single one of them! Ravindra told us that according to their tradition, they give the same mithai, so that it is easier to distribute it equally amongst relatives! I realized that tradition is sometimes based on good sense.

I wondered what their reaction was to the variety in the boxes we had left behind. Ravi was too polite to tell us even when we asked him in 2021; but he asked me to tell the story to their son, Raayaan. The story has become a part of our family lore.

~

At the time we were wandering in the by-lanes of Old Delhi, or Delhi-6 as it is now known, another young man, about Ravindra's age, was in Tihar Jail on the charge of being involved in bomb-blast cases. His name was Aamir Khan and he had been arrested and tortured and finally framed. It took Aamir over fourteen years to prove himself innocent, and by that time his father had died; his mother had had a stroke and could not speak.

I first heard of his situation from my colleague and fellow human-rights activist ND. Pancholi, who had taken up Aamir's case towards the end of the fourteen years. Aamir had been acquitted in all but one case, and he was out of jail. He wanted to tell his story and I agreed to write it for him.[16]

Aamir came to my home every morning and I would record his story. To begin with, he assumed I knew nothing about Old Delhi. He tried to present a picture of Old Delhi as a place representing syncretic culture where Hindus and Muslims fraternized and lived in harmony. But when I asked him which Hindu families he had visited, he finally admitted he had never been inside a Hindu home, even in his childhood, before he was framed.

Aamir said every morning his father would go out and have a cup of tea and chat to his friends. Then he would buy something to eat for breakfast for Aamir and his mother. I asked whether he remembered having bedmi and aloo sabzi or nagori–halwa. Aamir was stumped. He said he had grown up in the by-lanes of Old Delhi but had never heard of these delicacies. He refused to believe that I was talking about traditional food from his area. I showed him pictures on the Internet. He stared at the pictures of the little nagori puris made from semolina and heaps of halwa in utter disbelief. I, too, was shocked to learn that someone living in Old Delhi had never tasted these delicacies, which I thought of as being typically of Old Delhi.

I went to see an old friend from Jawaharlal Nehru University, Ranjana Saxena. She too was from Old Delhi. I asked whether she remembered eating nagori puri and halwa and her eyes lit up with the memories of her childhood. Then I asked whether Muslims also came to the same shop, and she said not as far as she could remember. 'We never went to each other's homes.' Amma had taken me to Old Delhi just before our ancestral homes were sold and that was when I had first tasted nagoris and bedmis. She had told me it was typical Old Delhi cuisine; she had not said it was Hindu cuisine, or that food was divided into Hindu and Muslim.

You can still find shops selling the classic bedmis and nagoris in Sitaram Bazar, Chandini Chowk—or you can get the bedmi mix online on Ebay! Today, this Hindu food has been secularized by the Internet. Many bloggers mention bedmis and nagoris, but none mention whether they are Hindu or Muslim. However, the Hindu and Muslim communities living in Delhi-6 continue to be deeply divided.

~

Every season in India and every festival are associated with special food. Till my Dadi was alive, we followed many of the traditions because she cooked the special dishes required for the occasion. We were also told about the special food cooked by other communities, such as the seviyan ki kheer on Eid-ul-Fitr. This festival's origins can be traced to the time of Prophet Mohammad. It is observed in the month of Shawwal, the tenth month in the Islamic calendar, a month after Ramzan, when Muslims fast.

Eid-ul-Fitr is often called 'meethi Eid', the sweet festival, synonymous with sweet seviyan. There are different kinds of seviyan or sheer khurma in South Asia and Central Asia. For instance, Anoothi Vishal states:

> Sheer Khurma, as the name suggests (sheer means 'milk'), is nothing but a kheer or milk pudding. Rice noodles are cooked in thickened milk to which dates (khurma refers to these) and other dried fruits are added to give a thick pudding. This is the most common seviyan preparation on Eid. The Kimami Seviyan, popular in Lucknow, Benares and other parts of the erstwhile Awadh, are a more elaborate preparation. Unlike

the sheer dessert, this one is dry, and loaded with ghee and dried fruits, including fried makhane (lotus seeds), raisins and other nuts, along with fragrant spices such as elaichi or green cardamom.[17]

One year when I was in Manipur in connection with a human-rights case, I was feeling homesick, and a friend from North India (a non-Muslim) and I made seviyan when we learnt it was Eid. It was a part of our shared culture. Many years later, when I was teaching at the Cochin University of Science and Technology (CUSAT), a friend, Zaida, and her husband, Hussain, invited me to their home for Eid.

I really loved Zaida ever since she told me her story of how she had got married to Hussain. She said her parents had married her to a man who was very learned and widely read, even though he was very poor. And it was true that her husband was truly well-read, and I learnt much from my wide-ranging interactions with him.

It was a festive mood that Eid, and I asked whether we would be eating seviyan. I was shocked when Hussain turned to me and said rather sternly: 'Islam has nothing to do with seviyan. Prophet Mohammad did not have seviyan, but dates.'

That was my first lesson in the distinction between Muslim culture and everyday faith, and the puritanical theology of political Islam.

Of course I knew that Prophet Mohammad did not eat kheer or seviyan; he had dates. His choice of food was dictated by the local context. In a literal interpretation of Islam, kheer became un-Islamic and only dates could be treated as authentic Islamic food. The literal interpretation ensures that all Muslims the world over break their fast with dates and water; the ritual is a means to unite Muslims across national and cultural boundaries; to homogenize them. A contextual interpretation of Islam, however, allows for diversity, and so unites the local Muslim community with its immediate cultural neighbours.

~

In an atmosphere of growing intolerance, every festival in India has become an occasion for instigating hatred and prejudice. In May 2017, Prashant Patel, a Gujarati Hindu advocate, posted on his Twitter account that Aligarh Muslim University does not serve lunch or dinner to Hindus during Ramzan. It was immediately proved to be fake news. But the episode demonstrated how food has become a weapon in the hands of religious fundamentalists and extremists. Some even speak of food fascism.

In such a climate, could culture and cuisines form a bridge between peoples belonging to different religions? Can appreciation and sharing of food become a way of forging friendships amongst diverse cultures and nations? How relevant was the upbringing

Amma and Papa had given me? Do those values they taught me have any relevance in the contemporary world?

I was about to start the long, long journey to try and find the answers…

3

FEMINIST FURIES

I cannot remember the names or dates, but this was the conversation between two children of my feminist friends: A little boy and a little girl were playing together. They were making rotis. The boy found it difficult and he said: 'It's a girl's job.' The girl replied: 'It is a question of experience.'

~

Amma did not insist that I learn cooking or any of the skills traditionally associated with girls and women. She herself could cook well and had knitted lovely little cardigans for her children; one I remember was with angora wool and had kittens on the pockets. She had had a sewing machine and would sew her own blouses. So it was not because she did not know how to cook, sew or knit that she had insisted I should not have to learn these things.

Amma had a strange theory: if her daughter did not have the skills required of a woman, then she could not be pushed into performing roles assigned to women. It was a way of ensuring I was free to choose the roles I wished to play

At school I had to take up Home Science, not out of choice, but because of a lack of it. In Home Science we had to learn many different skills, including cooking. And the teacher in charge was

Mrs Mathur who had joined Welham's from the first day of the school's opening in January 1957. But she had a liberal attitude to my hostility to learning a 'woman's role'.

Other girls baked cakes and custards; some made complicated vegetarian dishes, but I was given some simple tasks like making a cup of coffee or a tomato sandwich. Mrs Mathur passed me without much fuss; she had confidence that when the time came for the final examination I would study and get through.

I still remember the day I was asked to make a tomato sandwich. I thought it was really sporting of Mrs Mathur not to insist on my learning cooking, so I tried to make a really good job of the tomato sandwich. I put the sandwich in a cloth sandwich cover and served it to Mrs Mathur with a cup of Nescafe which I had made the way we had been taught: taking a spoon of sugar and coffee powder and a little warm water and whisking it with a teaspoon till it became all frothy; then hot water is poured into the cup, followed by a generous amount of milk and more sugar. That is the only coffee most of us knew since we had not tasted filter coffee or seen a coffee percolator.

Mrs Mathur looked at the sandwich and exclaimed: 'How can you make a mistake in a sandwich!' She was more amazed than angry. She discovered I had made not one mistake, but three! First, I had decorated the cover with bits of tomato and cucumber. This meant that when one opened the sandwich cover, the decoration would fall to the ground. Second, I had not cut the crust off the bread; and third, I had not put salt on the tomato.

~

I still find it odd that I should not have wanted to learn to bake or cook, especially since I actually enjoy cooking. I think this was a reaction to my father's sister and her idea that a woman's worth is to be judged only by her skills in cooking.

Saraswati Mushran, my father's sister and my Bua, was born in 1909. She was about five years older than Papa and had been married off to Kamta Prasad Mushran when she was barely out of her teens. Her father did not think it necessary to send girls to school and she was tutored at home. In fact, my grandfather did not send even his eldest son (my father) to school and insisted he was taught at home by a Sanskrit scholar. It was only on my grandmother's insistence that he went to school at the age of twelve or thirteen.

Bua had three daughters who had all been brought up like proper Kashmiri girls and were already married to proper Kashmiri men even before I had finished school. Her youngest was her son, Vinoo Bhai, who was (I thought) rather handsome and had bought me a jack-in-the-box when I was very little. He married Linnet, the maker of Bhuira jams.

I think Bua made up for her lack of formal education by mastering the traditional arts, especially cooking. Bua was a central figure in the Kashmiri community of Delhi. People came to her for advice on marriage alliances for their daughters, cooking lessons or to have a good old-fashioned gossip session. I remember how Bua would come to our home on Wellesley Road and put her plump hand near her mouth and gossip with her mother, my Dadi, who was barely sixteen years older than her. If there were people around they would gossip in zarzari or farfari, a secret language used by many Kashmiri women who prefix a 'zzz' sound or a 'ph' sound before every consonant.

When I was in boarding school in Dehra Dun and my parents were abroad, I had to spend my winter vacations with Bua because the government only paid the airfares for the summer vacations and Papa could not afford the fare for the shorter winter vacations.

It was an opportunity Bua seized upon, in the hope that she could re-model her brother's daughter and undo the damage that her sister-in-law Urmila had done. Bua did not like the fact that I had already reached my teens and did not know or, even worse, show any interest in cooking. Actually, her disapproval went far deeper. Bua blamed Amma for refusing to get my horoscope made by an astrologer; this would reduce my chances of getting a good husband. Before any match could be sanctified into a marriage, horoscopes had to be matched. Who would marry their son to a woman without a horoscope? I noticed she blamed my mother for these serious lapses and never my father, her brother.

Bua set about trying to make up for Amma's transgressions by getting me interested in cooking. She tried to win me over with love and warmth. But her oblique references to Amma's shortcomings made me feel a deep hostility which I expressed by refusing to enter her kitchen. My hostility was in part because it was Amma who always told me to love and respect Bua; she would not encourage my criticism of her.

Bua was not one to give up. She did wheedle me into learning how to make a perfect paan. I learnt to cut the betel nut into fine flakes with the traditional cutter, put just the right amount of katha and lime, then fold it to perfection and seal it with a clove. These paans would then be stuck on to silver toothpicks, laid on a silver tray with extra betel nuts and shown around to the guests after a meal.

~

Although I did not learn cooking from Bua, I did get my first lessons of how patriarchy functioned to divide women. I also felt angry because Bua reminded me that I was her brother's daughter and that was why she loved me. I wanted to be loved for being myself. Later, when I read feminist literature, I quickly understood many aspects of patriarchy because of these early experiences.

~

Papa had a reputation for being an excellent cook. He had even cooked a Kashmiri meal for the Indian delegation which formed a part of the Neutral Nations Repatriation Commission chaired by India. Papa was a member of the delegation and lived in a tent in the freezing cold Demilitarized Zone between North and South Korea, interviewing prisoners of war. I did not understand why he was in Korea but as a child I had seen photos of the anguished faces of the prisoners in his albums.

In the kitchen, Papa was like a true chef, temperamental and quick to get annoyed with any interference. But I did learn how to make koftas from him—putting oil on my palms and rolling the mince meat and coaxing it into cylindrical shapes; the trick is to apply even pressure.

Papa did not only cook Kashmiri food; his repertoire included a variety of European dishes, Kedgeree to Paella. He also made the biggest trifle pudding that I have seen—there were magical layers upon layers, beginning with eggless cake sponge so it could soak in the alcohol. Then there were fruits, jelly, cream and custard and sometimes bitter almonds. Papa was also especially famous for the massive omelettes he made almost every Sunday. The omelettes were soft and fluffy, stuffed with mushrooms or herbs and on occasion shrimps. His friends dropped in on Sunday mornings hoping to be on time for the omelette.

Of course, Papa was a good cook, but then so was Amma—except she did not have the same reputation.

Amma's repertoire was wide-ranging, from basic Kashmiri food to absolutely delicious ravioli and spaghetti bolognaise, which simply melted in the mouth. Many times I find myself longing for her chicken casserole and tamatar–aloo sabzi. She had trained our cooks, even Joseph, in Kashmiri cooking. But within the family Amma did not enjoy the same formidable reputation as Bua or Papa. I resented this deeply.

I am sure Amma did too.

I remember Amma asking us what we wanted for lunch or dinner; it was a question she asked every day and most days we would be irritated and ask her to decide. I could not understand why she was so resentful and could not decide what should be cooked. Now I understand only too well how annoying it is to have to decide on the menu twice a day, every day of your life. And it is a thankless task.

As a child, I knew Amma harboured deep resentment against a life where she could not realize her full potential. She did not understand institutionalized patriarchy the way my generation of feminists did. If Amma had read Betty Friedan's *Feminine Mystique* (1963) she would have identified with its central idea that women needed to find personal fulfilment outside their traditional roles. But she would have said that Betty Friedan did not deal with the wider forms of social inequality, oppression because of class, colonialism or imperialism.

For Amma, the narrative of difference between men and women was a kind of discrimination and inequality; she felt strongly about women's rights. But she was not familiar with concepts like gender and patriarchy. She would have dismissed Betty Friedan because Friedan was predominantly dealing with the problems of white middle-class women in the United States. Amma, and women of her generation, could not de-link the oppression of women from the wider struggle for the liberation of all human beings from class exploitation and imperialism. So

Amma continued to play her role as mother and wife, but would often complain: 'I am a doormat on which everyone wipes off their emotional dirt.'

In a perverse way, it was a protest of sorts that she never really let people know she could cook or even knit. And this attitude rubbed off on me; I refused to learn any of the skills women were supposed to have. And even when I could cook I would not tell anyone.

Many, many years later, I teased Amma that after she died I would not remember 'Maa ke haath ka khana', food cooked by my mother's hands. And she retorted: 'So that is the kind of feminist you are. You want to remember your mother only by the kind of food she cooked.'

I had a friend in Jawaharlal Nehru University who was an excellent cook. She said that after her marriage, whenever she went home, her father would ask her to cook something special for him. He would say very lovingly that he loved to eat food cooked by her hands. She said she hated being told to cook every time so she deliberately burnt the biryani and said she had forgotten how to cook. It was her protest. When I heard her story the first time, I was shocked—now it makes perfect sense!

~

One day, on a hot afternoon, my parents were resting in their air-conditioned bedroom and expressed a desire for tea. It was not yet four and the servants would come only by five. I offered to make tea. When they took the first sip of the tea I had made they nearly spat it out. It was so bitter! I had followed Amma's instructions, but instead of putting one teaspoon of tea leaves for each person I had put a heaped tablespoon for each person. But I did finally learn to make proper tea.

I still remember the day I made tea for the first time as an adult for my guests. I went into the kitchen and put the kettle on the stove and while I waited for the water to boil I set the tray. I took out the white tray cloth with delicate chikan embroidery and laid it on the tray; then I took out the tea cozy and the white and gold bone-china tea set—the teapot, the sugar bowl, the milk jug—and the little doily with beads to cover the milk jug. Then I took out the tea strainer and teaspoons and a smaller spoon for the sugar and, finally, the small napkin for holding the handle of the teapot.

The tray looked as beautiful as it had every morning when the servant brought it up for my parents' bed tea; except that in our home it was served not in the bedroom but on the large balcony of the first floor of our house, along with the newspapers. I can still see my parents sitting on the balcony overlooking the Chinese orange tree in a corner, or the bright red bottlebrush flowers blooming in summer and the green of the other trees which hid them from the neighbours.

The water had boiled and I poured a little bit into the pot and swirled it to warm the teapot and threw out the water. The tea was always Lipton Green Label Darjeeling tea. I put a teaspoon each for my two guests and myself into the pot and one extra for the teapot, just as my mother had taught me. I smiled as I remembered how I had put a tablespoon of tea leaves instead of a teaspoon.

I put the tea cozy on the teapot and lifted the tray and proudly carried it into the drawing room where my guests were waiting. I placed the tea tray on the coffee table and as I pulled off the cozy and poured the tea, I asked whether they would like strong tea or light. How much milk and how many teaspoons of sugar? I looked up waiting for an answer.

One of my guests was Jogen Sengupta, a Naxalite from Bengal. I had just begun my political life and this was perhaps my first meeting with a Naxal comrade. He looked at the tray and said with stern authority: 'Comrade Nandita, this is bourgeois tea. You must learn how to make proletarian tea.'

Of course, I knew that working-class people drank sweet, strong, milky tea. In our home the servants made theirs from the Red Label packet which was cheaper and stronger and brewed it with milk and sugar. I suddenly saw the truth behind Comrade Jogen's reprimand. It was an admonishment which I took to heart. I humbly asked how I should declass (the vocabulary of the Naxals) myself, and he told me that I must learn to make tea boiled with milk and sugar. I went meekly back to the kitchen carrying the tea tray and made my first cup of proletarian tea.

In that moment of humiliation, I suddenly felt anger that Comrade Jogen had neither offered to help me carry the tray nor help make the tea. It was my first feminist flash of anger.

I remembered the incident with Jogen when a young friend recently presented me with freshly picked tea from Darjeeling. She is from a working-class home and when I told her of Jogen's admonishment, she said her mother had friends among the tea-plantation workers who regularly brought fresh leaves for her. All of them liked the light tea and appreciating good tea had nothing to do with class. It was the packaging and the marketing that made it a bourgeois product.

A few days later Comrade Jogen committed his second mistake. He had invited himself to my house. I ignored his attitude and sense of entitlement and decided to make him kheer. I used a shortcut, which Amma had taught me—using Milkmaid condensed milk instead of standing and stirring the milk till it thickened. I felt it had turned out rather well. Jogen tried some and said in Bengali: 'The kheer is not like the one my mother cooks for me.'

~

I did not know it then but my Dadi, my father's mother, had suffered this kind of humiliation. I found this out from Papa's unpublished memoirs. He remembered the exact date on which the incident happened: 6 July 1929, a day before he left his father's home to go and study in Allahabad.

Dadi

> As I sat down, I saw my father take a knife in his hand and join my mother in peeling potatoes. When he had finished a single potato and was cutting it into pieces, he took in his hand a small bit and told my mother that the pieces she had cut were a little too large for stuffing into a karela. My mother retorted with traces of pain in her voice that my father was never happy with anything she did…

My father went away to Allahabad and then to London for further studies and he recalls that when he returned after seven years, his mother told him:

> 'Do you know that at one stage when you were away for nearly seven years in England, I took the courage to tell your father that his constantly finding fault with me, especially with my

> cooking, and comparing it to my disadvantage with that of his mother, was unfair. I then uttered a sentence which had a profound effect on your father during the last decade of our life together. I said that he never seemed to realize that he had married me, and not his mother.

Papa writes that Dada bought Dadi an exquisite sari and thereafter 'he was a changed character'.

~

The experience with Comrade Jogen was my first encounter with deeply entrenched patriarchy within the Naxalite movement. And I would suffer humiliation again and again; and each time I would end up blaming myself, thinking that I was overreacting to small, irrelevant incidents instead of focusing on the larger picture. But my resentment kept building up. It was the beginning of my feminist consciousness and understanding the insidious ways in which patriarchy worked to undermine women's self-respect and dignity.

In the 1970s I was active in the autonomous women's movement which was deeply influenced by feminist ideas. It was called 'autonomous' because it was not linked to any political party, though most of the ideological leaders at the time were women with leftist backgrounds; many had withdrawn from the left parties because at the time there was little room within the parties for independent, thinking women.

I was by then a journalist working with the *Indian Express*. But I left journalism and took to law because we were finding it very difficult to find lawyers who could defend women's rights in the courts. I went for law classes in the evenings and in the mornings I would participate in the women's movement.

After I graduated, I joined a law firm called J.B. Dadachanjee and Company. On one of my first assignments I accompanied the clients to the chamber of a senior lawyer who lived in Defence Colony. After a little while, a huge tray with tea and accompanying snacks was brought in by a servant who looked around wondering where to place it. The senior advocate smiled and indicated that the tray should be placed in front of me—I was the only woman present in the room.

I pretended I did not understand. The conference continued and I ignored the tray. Finally, the senior advocate looked at me, and again with a smile asked me to make the tea. I looked at him and in a respectful tone said firmly: 'I did not join a law firm to pour tea.'

The senior advocate was obviously taken aback; but he got up and went inside and brought his grandson. The boy was still in his Modern School uniform. The boy looked at me and asked, 'How do I make the tea?' This time I did not protest, but instructed the boy on how to make a cup of tea. I told him to ask each one how much sugar they wanted and to hand each one the cup.

The matter was reported to Dadachanjee, but to his credit, he did not feel it necessary to tell me to mend my ways.

~

Although I had joined law in order to take up women's rights, I found that the women's organizations were not willing to trust a junior lawyer with their cases. Instead, the first cases I received were human-rights cases.

I began my serious involvement with the human-rights movement in the early 1980s. I soon found that the majority of activists were men with no understanding of patriarchy or women's rights. I found myself arguing their cases in the Supreme Court in the mornings and cooking for them in the evenings, since they stayed at my flat in Munirka Enclave when they came to Delhi. At the time I did all the housework, mainly because I could not afford any help.

When I protested, the men had different reactions. As human-rights activists they could not question the political basis of my protests, but they would not change their ways. Balagopal (1952–2009) was General Secretary of the Andhra Pradesh Civil Liberties Committee (APCLC). His solution was to quietly go out and eat in some dhaba. Sujata Bhadra, the Secretary General of the Bengal-based Association for the Protection of Democratic Rights (APDR), tried to cook and he nearly blew up the pressure cooker.

The only activists who never expected me to cook for them were the Nagas, most of whom I had met while studying at the Jawaharlal Nehru University, Delhi. The Naga students there had formed their own human-rights organization, the Naga People's Movement for Human Rights (NPMHR), and one of the first cases I filed on their behalf was against the Indian armed forces for committing human-rights violations during counter-insurgency operations. This was when I discovered that in democratic India we had a law which allowed the government to impose virtual army rule in parts of the country.

My mother was convinced that my commitment to the Naga cause was because of my love of their food! In part, perhaps, it was, but it was also because the Naga activists I met did not expect me to cook and wash their dishes.

On one occasion, I went to Patiala on the invitation of a friend, Veena Nabar. I had been introduced to her by her husband, comrade Manmohan, but soon we had our independent relationship and she came to see me whenever she was in Delhi. She said she loved Mohan, and if he was a character in a novel, he would be always loveable. But she was frustrated and angry with the way he and other male comrades treated their wives. She said it was doubly difficult to criticize the husbands because they were also comrades and a criticism of them would implicitly be a criticism of their work as communists.

Veena and the other women comrades had another problem. Because the men refused to share in the housework or look after the children, the women could not participate in political activities. Veena invited me to Patiala to talk to the women (mainly wives of male comrades) and discuss what could possibly be done. She said since so many of the men were my clients, they would accept my talking to their wives.

It was an extraordinary meeting at the time. The women were happy to be able to pour out their feelings. When we came out of our meeting we found all the husbands sitting outside, looking really tense. We all had a laugh. After all, we were comrades!

The last time I met Veena she had become a lawyer and Manmohan was working with children, showing them magic tricks.

I travelled to Hyderabad on several occasions during this time, and I found there were intense debates between the feminists and the male human-rights activists. But what was extraordinary was that though the words were very sharp, the personal relations between the two were warm and always friendly. One famous Naxalite poet, Vara Vara Rao, had written a poem from inside prison talking about the long wait for freedom, and a feminist had responded that the woman's wait was never-ending; she did not get freedom at the end of her daily waiting on her husband or her children.

I often stayed in the home of Vasantha and K.G. Kannabiran in Hyderabad. Vasantha is a feminist scholar and poet, and

Kannabiran, who passed away in 2010, was a human-rights lawyer. It was at their home and among their friends and fellow comrades that I heard the fierce debates, but always in a most humane and democratic manner.

I learnt a lot from Vasantha about caring for people and that as feminists, we could combine our desire to care and to mother with our right to recognition as individuals. We often had these discussions over delicious food. One of the dishes I really liked was Vasantha's 'fried egg on dosa'. It was such a good idea!

Once, when Balagopal was arrested and Kannabiran and I were going to meet him, Vasantha came with us in solidarity with me. I remember saying on the way, 'I love Balagopal and all these activists, but I would never marry any one of them!'

Kannabiran teased me: 'Not even me?'

With Kannabiran and Balagopal.

I remained silent. He was joking, making light of my remark, and I let it be. I did not explain that I wanted to marry someone who would share the housework *and* my commitment to human-rights work.

P.A Sebastian of the Committee for the Protection of Democratic Rights (CPDR) came up with the idea of setting up an all India Human Rights Tribunal, with the secretaries of the human-rights groups from different states becoming the core team. This team included K. Balagopal, Sujata Bhadra and myself.

The first case we took up was the police firing in Arwal, Bihar on 19 April 1986. Siding brazenly with a powerful landlord, the police had shot down 21 landless workers. We had persuaded former judges of the Supreme Court and various High Courts and they had agreed to be on the Tribunal. T.U. Mehta, former Chief Justice of the Himachal Pradesh High Court, and P.S. Poti, former Chief Justice of the Gujarat High Court, sat on the Tribunal and gave their report, which was released in Calcutta on 30 July 1987 by the famous filmmaker Mrinal Sen.

We had all worked very hard, but I had felt that as the only woman in the team, I faced problems which needed to be addressed. For instance, when we were travelling and stayed with friends or comrades in their homes, their wives expected me to help in the kitchen; they did not expect the men to do so. As the only trained lawyer (when Sebastian was not there) I had to also do a lot of drafting, so I needed to be left alone. The wives would resent the fact that I was treated differently from them, and I did not like being pitted against other women.

At home, too, I would vacillate between wanting to cook and care for the activists, whom I considered comrades, and throwing them out of the house if they refused to work. By then I had read enough feminist literature to understand my predicament and decided I ought to fight for my own rights. Balagopal supported me. I called for a formal meeting to discuss the issues, and we all met after the release of the report in Calcutta at the home of Rajashri Dasgupta and her husband, Sushil Khanna.

The activists revered Rajashri Dasgupta because she had been a Naxalite and had suffered torture and imprisonment. Now she was married to a professor and had a little son. She had the radiance of motherhood and looked kind and serene. My heart sank when she said she had cooked beef just the way Balagopal liked it. How were these male activists or perhaps even Rajashri going to react to my complaints?

The meeting began in the drawing room with Rajashri sitting on the floor with her son. I explained the problem and said it was not a 'personal problem' but a political one. To my relief Rajashri spoke out clearly and unequivocally for me and that ended the meeting. The human-rights activists gathered there—all male except for me—acknowledged the problem, but did not think it necessary to find a solution. Finding a solution would have entailed changing their own attitudes towards women; coming to grips with patriarchy and dismantling it. So the meeting ended peaceably, everyone felt good and enjoyed the beef and rice, and I knew nothing had changed.

Over time, however, many of the women in the Naxalite movement and those close to the party did influence the movement to change its understanding of the role of women, and to also understand patriarchy and its relationship to caste and class. One of them was Anuradha Gandhy (1954–2008), a graduate in sociology from the prestigious Elphistone College, Bombay. Anuradha's father was a high-profile Bombay lawyer and both her parents had been communists. Anuradha was in the central committee of one of the Naxalite groups, the highest decision-making body in the Communist Party, and had drafted a paper on Naxalism and Feminism.

I spent one night at her home in Nagpur in December of 1984, by which time she was already a full-time party worker. I had gone with a fact-finding team into the forests of Gadchiroli and had come back tired; she made me comfortable and heated water for a hot bath. I sat up the whole night writing out the report on the conditions of the tribals and the atrocities committed by the police.

When I got up in the morning, I found her already making breakfast and I asked what she was cooking. She said: 'Poha.' I said I wanted to learn and she turned out to be a good teacher. I still remember the way she taught me, and I have made poha often since then. In fact, whenever I make poha I remember the day I spent with this remarkable woman and revolutionary. I felt a sense of personal loss when I heard the news in April 2008 that she had died of falciparam malaria. A few years later, her husband and comrade, Kobad Gandhy, was arrested when he came to Delhi for treatment for cancer.

~

In 1988, I went to Imphal to fight a case on behalf of a Naga human-rights organization. I was staying at the guesthouse of the Manipur Baptist Church (MBC). The case involved brutalities committed by the Assam Rifles during a counter-insurgency operation, codenamed Operation Bluebird.[18] The armed forces had tortured to death many men, raped women and girls and destroyed property in and around the village of Oinam in Senapati district, Manipur—the home of the Poumai Naga tribe. Among the most horrendous of the acts of savagery was forcing two pregnant women to give birth to their babies in an open playground.

One day I returned exhausted from court and asked Paul Leo to make me a cup of tea. Paul, a Poumai Naga, was from Oinam village and his uncles had been tortured to death; at the time he was a law student studying in Delhi University. Paul said he did not know how to make tea and he went next door and asked one of the evangelists, Ruth, to make it for me. I was furious. I said if I could fight for his people, why could he not make a cup of tea without asking another woman to do so? Ruth, a Tangkhul Naga woman, tried to pacify me. She said she did not mind making the tea for me. Of course, that was not the point. But nothing I said made any sense to her. She was not remotely aware of the women's movement or feminism.

Soon thereafter, Aram Pamei arrived. She was the Women's Secretary of the MBC, and had a better understanding of my arguments. She promised to explain to a very confused Ruth why I was so angry. I do not think Ruth fully understood. It would be many years before Naga women spoke out against patriarchy.

Aram Pamei was a single woman and had studied theology in Bangalore and also in South Korea. I shared Aram's small room in the MBC for almost a year, and it was our feminism which united us, the evangelist and the non-believer.

Aram told me she wanted to study feminist theology and she was pleased when I presented her the two-volume *The Women's Bible* written by Elizabeth Cady Stanton (1815–1902). I had brought the book for her from America when I went there to lobby with the Human Rights Committee on the Armed Forces (Special Powers) Act. *The Women's Bible* challenged the traditional religious orthodoxy that women should be subservient to men.

I suggested to Aram that she do research under Gabriele

Dietrich, a feminist theologian teaching at the Tamil Nadu Theological Seminary at Madurai, where they had a Department of Social Analysis. But the Baptist church refused Aram permission.

Sharing a meal with Aram at the MBC guesthouse in Imphal.

A few days later, one of the student leaders, Somipem, came to my room and with a wicked smile on his face asked, 'Would you like a cup of tea?' When I said yes, please, he enquired, 'Would you like me to ask Ruth to make a cup of tea for you?' So, the story had gone around about my feminist fury! They could not really understand what the storm in the teacup was all about. As usual, it seemed that my assertion of my rights as a woman was small and petty in comparison to the human rights of so many.

~

After the Oinam case was over, I took up a temporary job teaching at the Cochin University of Science and Technology. I was given the rank of Reader and was teaching a paper on humanitarian and refugee law. I was put up at the guesthouse, but no arrangements were made for my food. When I asked the head of department, Chandrashekhar Pillai, what arrangements were being made for food, the professor replied: 'Don't you cook at home?'

I asked him that if a male teacher had been there in my place would he also be expected to cook his own meals? If they could not make arrangements for me, I would pack my bags and leave.

Arrangements were made forthwith and I continued to teach. But I discovered that I was teaching against a reserved post. In order not to appoint a permanent teacher, who would be a Dalit, they had employed me. Under such circumstances I could not continue for a second term.

~

You may have got the impression that I do not like cooking or that I cannot cook. In fact, I like cooking and feeding people when they come to my home. And it has been wonderful that I have a husband who also loves to cook and to eat.

Sebastian at the table.

In part, it was food that brought Sebastian and me together. We have now been married for more than a quarter of a century, and before that we had worked together for a decade. And the best times have been cooking and sharing a meal together—while fighting against the violation of human rights, from the Northeast to Kashmir.

Sebastian's love of food and cooking came from his father,

Luichumhao Hongray. His father was, like his son, a man of few words. Yet even without words, he was the one person who accepted me as I am and showed his love and acceptance by cooking something special for me. On one occasion, when I got up at five in the morning and went to the kitchen in Ukhrul, I found he had made fresh plum jam and small egg puffs for breakfast. He quietly smiled when he saw the delight on my face. On another occasion, he made melt-in-the-mouth beef balls cooked in milk with soft parathas, which he packed and gave us for dinner. I wanted so much to include his recipe for the meat balls but no one in the family remembered it and none of us had bothered to write it down. We always take our parents for granted till it is too late.

Sebastian's father could also cook really good Italian food which he had learnt from the Italian priests with whom he had

My father-in-law making parathas.

worked. He cooked for them and earned enough to give his children a good education. But he did not really like to teach; he was impatient with people asking too many questions, so the only way to learn was to watch.

Every single day he would rise at four in the morning and light the fire and make tea for everyone. He cooked all the meals. Once, when he was still well, I asked him to come and stay with us in Bangalore and he was quite keen. But Sebastian's mother asked: 'If you go who will cook?'

Sebastian's mother is also a good cook, but she just did not like doing it on a daily basis.

~

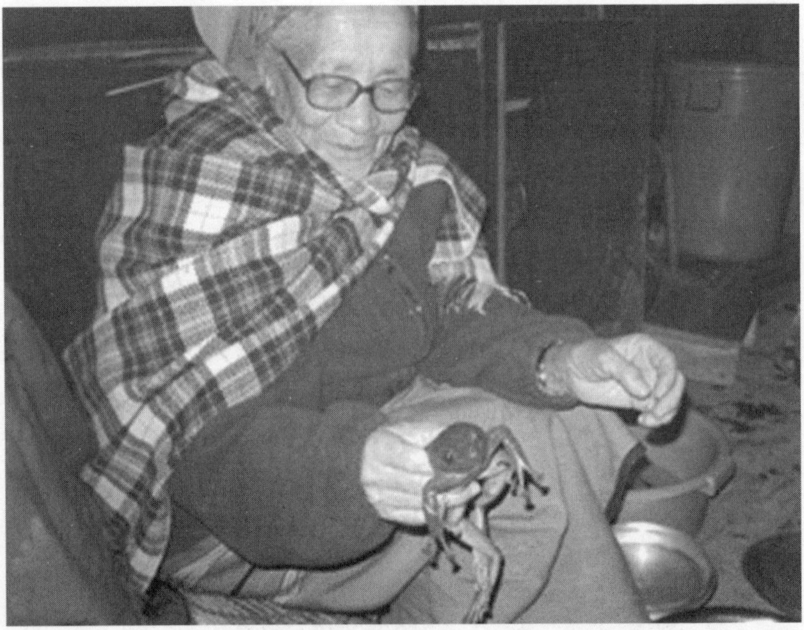

My mother-in-law cooking in her kitchen in Ukhrul.

Sebastian and I loved to experiment with food. Bano Haralu, a friend living in Guwahati, once asked Sebastian to buy some beef for her; Bano's mother was visiting her from Nagaland and she wanted five kilos of meat. But when Sebastian arrived with the beef he found that Bano's mother had already left for Kohima, and so we were left with a lot of beef.

That was when I remembered the delicious non-vegetarian pickles we used to buy in Himachal Pradesh. It was usually chicken and pork pickle, but I thought I couldn't go wrong if I made beef pickle instead. I remembered Amma saying that a good cook should be able to reproduce a dish just by smelling it. It was like my dance teacher, who expected us to reproduce certain dance steps only by listening to the sound of ghungroos, or ankle-bells. So I recalled memories of the Himachal pickle and decided on the ingredients for our beef pickle.

At the time we were living in a flat above the Christian Literature Society in Guwahati's Paan Bazar. It was within the Mission Compound so we had access to the cheerful labour of several children of our friends! We called two of the children to help us peel garlic and slice green chillies. We boiled the beef with a bit of salt and haldi, mixed the garlic and green chillies, and put it all in a jar and poured fresh mustard oil into it. We kept the pickle in the sun for a week and voilà! There was our beef achaar. By the time we had shared it with all our friends we had only a small bottle left—and I got a reputation for being a good cook.

~

Sebastian and I had a civil marriage with the Registrar coming over to Sebastian's uncle's home in Imphal. For many of our guests this was the first time they had seen a civil marriage, without religious rites and rituals.

We went up to Ukhrul for a blessing by a Catholic priest. This was the difficult part because I insisted that the words of the blessing must not be against my feminist principles of equality; also that the words must be in consonance with Christian values. The priest was a Naga and we worked out a blessing which took into account our religious and political sensibilities; and he blessed our differences. It turned out to be a moving ceremony and I think we set a precedent. But it is a precedent that cannot be followed since the majority of Tangkhul Nagas are Baptists who do not allow a marriage between even Catholics and Baptists, let alone between a Baptist and a pagan!

I do not know how many guests came for our wedding in Ukhrul; but it was a community affair in which a great many people participated to make a memorable celebration. The youth belonging to the Hongray clan constructed the stage in the open grounds, and relatives and family cut two pigs and a buffalo presented by Sebastian's sisters for the feast, as was the custom.

I do not know how many kilos of salt and chilli powder were put in the curries; but I do know that the two big, fat pigs were not enough to feed all the guests. So a friend, Sam, rushed to his village and brought a pig; he also brought a busload of guests who he thought should have been invited from other villages or Imphal!

The cooking for festivals is done by men in the Tangkhul Naga community, as is done in the Kashmiri community. The difference is that among the Tangkhuls there were no professional cooks, whereas in the Kashmiri community we had professional cooks who were all men.

The old mother of a friend came to me and apologized for not bringing her own bowl of cooked rice. I could not understand the context and Sebastian explained that it was the custom for the neighbours to bring their own cooked rice to eat with the curries. In the midst of this chaos, Sebastian's youngest sister did not forget to cook a special meal for Mamu and our other friends who did not eat pork or beef. She made chicken and fish for them, and fried vegetables.

There was singing and a local comedian came in the evening and entertained us for hours till we were all exhausted from eating and laughing.

~

Just after we got married, we were sitting in Chingmeirong in Sebastian's uncle's place in Imphal. We called him Uncle Hongray. That day, there was no one besides the three of us, and Uncle wondered who would cook the dinner. I volunteered. Uncle was silent. Then he told Sebastian in Tangkhul: 'She does not put chillies.'

Sebastian said he could tell me to put chillies and that I could cook. I decided to cook fish with fermented bamboo shoot. Uncle Marius Hongray was surprised that the dish was to his liking and he even told family members that I could cook well!

Uncle Hongray

My best memory of Uncle Hongray is of him inviting me to share the rice beer he was drinking from his bamboo cup. I felt finally accepted. He passed away a few years ago. In memory of Uncle Hongray, here is the recipe of the fish I cooked for him.

FISH WITH FERMENTED BAMBOO SHOOT

Ingredients

- 1 kg rahu fis
- 1 tomato (chopped)
- 1 onion (preferably ground)
- Panch phoran masala: mix together a pinch of these five seeds: fenugreek (methi dana), nigella (kalonji), cumin (jeera), black mustard (rai), fennel (sauf)
- A large bay leaf
- Haldi (turmeric powder) Salt
- 2 green chillies (slit)
- Smoked red chillies (optional)
- Fermented Bamboo shoots (not more than five-six pieces)
- Mustard oil
- Fresh coriander

Method

- Coat the fish pieces with haldi and salt and fry till golden brown. In the same oil (if there is extra oil take out some) put the panch phoran masala taking care that it does not burn. Just after it stops spluttering, put in the bay leaf and the onion (preferably ground). After the onion is fried, put in the tomato pieces and the slit green chillies and the red chillies, haldi and a little salt. Put the fermented bamboo shoots or bamboo water. Pour water depending on how thick you want the gravy, and let the mixture boil. After it boils, put in the fried fish pieces and let it simmer to the consistency you want. Garnish with fresh green coriander.
- Serve hot with steamed rice.

Over the years I have invented many recipes for an Indo-Naga cuisine. One of the most successful has been smoked brinjal with fermented fish:

SMOKED BRINJAL WITH FERMENTED FISH

Ingredients

- One fermented fish (available online and in shops selling Northeast food)
- One round brinjal
- 2–3 pods garlic
- 4–5 green chillies or one umrok (Raja chilli)
- A spoonful of mustard oil
- Salt

Method

- Wash and dry the brinjal and rub it well with the mustard oil
- Put the brinjal directly on a low flame and let the skin become black, like done for begun bharta.
- Boil the green chillies/umrok or roast them on the fire
- Peel off the skin of the brinjal.
- Boil or roast one fermented fis
- Grind the garlic pods to a paste
- Mix all the ingredients well with a fork or fry them in a little oil. The chutney is ready.

~

There is something about my Naga friends and acquaintances that still makes me angry, though. It is the way that the Naga women, even those we do not know well, want to take over my kitchen when they visit us. No one asks where to put things or which pan to use, or which cloth to wipe with. It comes from their feeling of being superior to women like me who do not have children. It is beyond their imagination that any woman can choose not to have children.

And I feel sad that I cannot have the types of conversations with them, share jokes and anecdotes, that I can with my feminist friends. But Naga women, as I've noted earlier, are now becoming aware of the fact that their society is patriarchal and they need to question customs and attitudes. I was so pleased when I had occasion to have some open conversations with our Tangkhul Naga friends John and Nelly when we stayed in their home in Dehra Dun some time ago. Nelly said she liked having us as guests because we did not expect her to serve us and we were not formal.

Her husband, John, had organized a meeting in their house with the Nagas studying and working in Dehra Dun. The meeting was to discuss my book *The Exodus Is Not Over: Migrations from the Ruptured Homelands of the Northeast*. Nelly had shown particular interest in the problems faced by women working in the beauty industry. But when the meeting started, Nelly was not there. She was in the kitchen, even though she had so much wanted to be a part of the discussion. When tea was served, a woman student got up to serve the cake. I objected and pointed out that this was not necessarily a female job. It was just a few weeks previously that women in Nagaland had demanded implementation of reservations for women in the Legislative Assembly, and the men had gone on a rampage and burnt down property. The images posted on Facebook were fresh in everyone's mind. Everyone laughed (albeit nervously) in response to my objection and a male student got up to serve the cake.

After the meeting, when the guests had left, I pointed out to Nelly how gender inequality works. But what was the alternative, she asked. 'It is my duty to cook.' I shared with her our well-rehearsed feminist alternatives; she could cook in the morning or a day earlier so that she could join similar discussions and meetings. We could also have open kitchens, so that the woman could be a part of the discussions. And, of course, the work could—should—be equally shared between the spouses.

Nelly listened carefully, then said: 'But I like playing the role of mother and wife, because that is what it says in the Bible.' I deferred for another time a discussion with her on feminist theology, which has challenged patriarchal interpretations of the Bible.

~

But Nagas have the last word on the origins of inequality between the sexes and the sufferings of women: If Adam and Eve had been Nagas, they would have left the apple untouched and eaten the snake!

~

Many Naga women are beginning to resent having to do all the housework. And in the cities and towns of Nagaland and in the Naga areas of Manipur, families employ children as servants. Even in the meeting at John and Nelly's home, a student leader from the Khiamniungan Naga tribe told us about the abuse of children from his community who are working in homes of Nagas living in Kohima, Dimapur and other towns. He said two children had been found dead recently. He asked what could be done.

I had myself seen how little children are abused by their Naga employers and had been shocked; especially when I saw the way a pastor and his wife exploited a little girl of five. The children are sent to town in the hope they will be able to get some education, but they are not even given proper accommodation or food.

In Nagaland, a fledgling organization of domestic workers has been formed, affiliated to the National Domestic Workers Union. The Union has been fighting to extend the protection of labour law to domestic workers.

~

For a long time, Sebastian and I did not employ any domestic workers and did the work ourselves. But in 1996 I fell ill and things had to change.

As happens with most people when they fall ill, I became a victim of unsolicited advice from almost everyone who came to see me—and most gave their advice before finding out what was wrong with me. Some Naga friends brought me leaves and herbs and one even gave me bear's bile. I was told it was a cure for everything.

But the most tyrannical of these quacks were some of my feminist friends who were committed to alternative forms of medicine, swearing that they never took Western medicine (until they got severely ill, of course). One of them told me to gargle with cod-liver oil and when I said I could not bear it, she told me that it was because I did not want to get well. This was a fundamentalist kind of feminism, which is as intolerant as religious fundamentalism.

My father asked the Head of Hamdard Dawakhana to have a look at me. He felt my pulse and said the cause of my illness was the anger burning inside me. He probably came close to understanding what I was feeling. I had recently been involved in a court battle against the privatization of the telecom sector and had seen and been outraged by how the public sector had been sold to multinational corporations for a song.

This was interesting, because the Ayurveda doctor whom we went to later also asked me whether I felt a lot of anger. I wondered how he knew, but my joints were paining too much for me to try to understand the principles of Ayurvedic medical science. Finally, armed with medicines from Kottakkal Vaidyashala, painkillers and steroids, Sebastian and I sold our flat in Delhi and moved to Goa, to a flat on the island of Chorao.

It was in Chorao that we first employed a maid to help with our housework. And as time passes and we grow old, our dependence on these wonderful women grows. They have provided us with love, care and succour when they are in need of those things much, much more than we are. I am amazed that they can wish me so cheerfully when they have so much pain in their hearts. They cook, wash, clean and dust and, after making fabulous food for my guests, carry home a few leftovers from our dining table because however much they work, there is never enough for their own children.

I tell many of them that I would like to write their stories and they are pleased with the idea; but then they say they do not have time to sit and talk to me. Yet, I still feel that the least I can do is to record some of their experiences.

~

Nanda came to work for us soon after we moved to Chorao. She used to come with a smile on her face and flowers in her hair. Her husband was a tailor, but he had a weak heart so could no longer provide for their small family, and she was the sole breadwinner. It was Nanda who gave us our first taste of authentic Goan food and her stuffed mackerels were absolutely fabulous.

Some days, when Nanda missed the only bus from her locality, she walked some three kilometres and then worked in a neighbour's house and then ours. One day, I asked Nanda whether she would like one of the massive tin trunks I had in which I had brought my books. It was lying on the verandah. She said she would and she hired a tempo to take the trunk to her place. As the tempo left, there was a knock on the front door. It was my Punjabi neighbour, Mrs Pasricha, and she was irate: how dare I give such gifts, and by giving Nanda better wages I had already created problems for everyone. Now all the maids would start demanding more money… I was flabbergasted.

The next day, Nanda came with tears in her eyes. She said Mrs Pasricha had shouted at her and now she would only be working for me. I replied that I did not want to be accused of stealing her and be on bad terms with my neighbour. That was when Nanda got angry and it was the only time I saw her in a rage. 'I have a right to work *wherever* I want. And why should *you* be afraid? Is she a relative that you have to be afraid of her?'

My neighbour spread the word among the richer residents of the locality that I was a terrible person; Nanda countered by telling the poorer residents that it was my neighbour who was evil, I was the good one.

On one occasion, when I returned from Delhi, Nanda turned up. Her eyes were full of sadness, she no longer had flowers in her hair and she looked thinner. Her husband had died and now she was at the mercy of his relatives. When I visited her home, I saw she had been given a tiny room next to the kitchen without a window. Her husband's brother had occupied the house.

The last time I saw Nanda was when she came to my home in Panaji. She brought laddoos and was wearing a nice sari. She came to say her son Gautam—the love of her life—had graduated and got a job as a cashier in a casino. But she rarely sees him since he works all night and she has to work in the mornings.

Manisha, who works for us in Delhi, is a petite woman who loves to dress up, and some days I get a whiff of perfume. When she first came to work for us I was thrilled to find she was from Lucknow. She has all the quiet dignity and etiquette of a lady from Lucknow.

One day I sat down with her and declared my love for her; and she said she too liked me. And so she has stayed on. And as the years go, she has revealed herself and the more I know the greater the respect I have for her.

Manisha lives in Najafgarh with her daughter and two sons. It is more than twenty kilometres from our flat in Vasant Enclave and she travels by bus, changing twice. After working for us, she walks some ten minutes to cook for the children of another family, and then walks to Anand Niketan, another twenty minutes, crossing a busy road, to cook for a third family. In other words, she cooks for her own family and for three other families every single day. She returns home around nine at night and then warms up the leftovers for herself and the children.

The amazing part is that every day she makes us tea, lunch and dinner with the same care and the taste is consistently good. Her soft, melt-in-the-mouth parathas are famous and she never complains, even when she has to make dozens of them for our guests. On some days when she is tired I call for pizzas (vegetarian and hot for her, meaty and bland for me) and we chat.

She says her parents married her off to a man who does little work and spends whatever he earns in his little shop on alcohol. When her children were small, she would bring them to work. Life was very difficult and there was little security, but she could not afford to give up.

She promised her children that she would work hard so that they could get a good education, and she would look after all their needs. But she had one condition—they must never tell her lies. She has now fulfilled her promise and her eldest child is a graduate. She has also managed to buy a plot of land and build a house. The house does not as yet have a water connection, though, and she and the boys have to fetch drinking water from the tanker which comes to their area once a week. The struggle is far from over.

~

Many of the women who have worked in our homes in Delhi and Goa were victims of domestic violence. For instance, Martha, who came to work for us in Goa for only a few weeks.

Martha was a dwarf. She always wished us a bright good morning and if we gave her anything, even the leftover food, she accepted it with gratitude and a prayer of thanks in the kitchen. Looking at her I would never have guessed the extent of her pain and suffering or the rage within her.

When she agreed to work for us, she had said that I would have to give her time off on days when she would need to go to court for her husband's trial. I learned the details a few days later. She told me that her husband used to rape their daughters when she was at work. Some days, when she came back home after cooking in three houses, he would not let her in. She would spend hours banging on the door and begging to be let in; and then the brute would let her in only to beat her.

Martha had three daughters and she waited till they grew up before taking any action. Once they were older, she complained to the police and got the man arrested. He was now in jail begging her to take him out on bail. But she was determined to get him convicted. This was why she never missed a single date in court.

One day, she told me her daughter had finished school and was now going to college. She needed eight thousand rupees for her admission and did not know where it would come from. She did not ask for the money. When I gave it to her, her gratitude was so profound that I felt a deep sense of shame.

There were other horror stories. Sandhya, who was also with us—in Delhi—for only a few weeks, was from Madhya Pradesh and was married to a Goan Catholic. She had the build of a wrestler and her hands were powerful. She had two skills: cooking and massaging. She had left her job in Jawaharlal Nehru University because her employer there had given her the job of a cook but expected free massages.

In the short time she was with us, she told me her story. Her husband worked as a security guard, so he had to be away all night, and she worked in several homes, mostly as a cook. This meant she had to leave her son alone in the house. On one occasion when she went back home after her last shift, she found that her little son had been sodomized by a neighbour.

She told me she did not think of going to the police. 'It would have been no use; criminals never get punished.'

The boy had changed after the trauma, she said, she could see terror in his eyes.

~

Perhaps the person I loved the most was Hila, a Zeliang Naga from Nagaland.

Hila had fallen in love with a Chin refugee from Myanmar but her family did not approve of their relationship, so she eloped with him. He took her to Myanmar. It was a journey fraught with danger and she had neither a passport nor a visa. This was during army rule in that country, so she had to hide when the police or army came to check the house where they were living, because all visitors had to be registered at the police station.

Some years later, the couple moved to Delhi. Hila's husband used to work at a private hospital as an interpreter for Chin patients who needed treatment but did not know English. Then one day he had a fight at the hospital and left the job. He had heard that I was doing the Burmese refugee cases and he sent me a SMS: 'I need a job, we are starving.' We were in Delhi at the time and we hired him as a help at home.

However, after working for a few days he brought his wife and said that she would work instead of him. That was how Hila came into our lives. But she said she did not want to be a maid. She wanted to spend her entire time looking after her three children.

Her husband drank heavily and got into fights with other Chins. We were in Goa when Hila, pregnant with a fourth child, took a train and came to us in Goa. Her husband complained to her brother that she had run off and her brother took her husband's side. Hila cried all night and returned to Delhi.

Her husband then told her he had a job to do in U.P. and he would be back soon. But he abandoned her and their four kids. Yet, Hila refused to believe that she was now a single mother, abandoned by the man she had married in the teeth of opposition. She left work with us soon after, so that she could be with the kids. The last time I contacted her, she was still waiting for her husband to return.

~

Then there is Annapurna. She is from Karnataka but has lived in Goa for decades. She too had a love marriage and she and her husband came to Goa in search of livelihood. When they came they had no money. Annapurna says 'a kind man' helped them by giving them work at a construction site. The two worked as construction workers.

Someone spotted her at the construction site one day and offered her a job as a maid. Since then, she has been working as a maid and cook. She has worked for people from all over India, so when I ask her to cook something she says, 'Remind me how you like it cooked. I cook for so many different people I forget what each one wants.' She told me her husband gets angry because she puts too little chilli in the curry—the result, she says, of working many years for white people.

Some years ago, her husband had an accident, and they went back to their village and stayed there for a year till he was able to walk again. Now he cannot do heavy work. He works as a gardener. He also has another job: a lady has employed him to feed stray dogs in her neighbourhood. She has even given him a second-hand car to carry the food, usually chicken and rice, for the dogs.

Annapurna and I have one serious point of conflict: she just hasn't learnt to make a nice 'English' cup of tea with very little milk and sugar. One day, I got really angry and refused to drink the milky tea she put in front of me; and she threatened to leave my service. I said she could go. But we had a truce. I no longer ask her to make Green Label Darjeeling tea. (Yes, Comrade Jogen, I have gone back to my upper-class tea!) She prefers the strong Red Label Tea, with lots of milk and sugar.

Annapurna.

Annapurna is now a grandmother. She may not know how to make Darjeeling tea but she has not stopped learning, facing life's challenges. Last week, when I opened the door for her, her face was lit up. She had learnt how to ride a two-wheeler! She now drives herself to my house.

~

I am sure all these women working as domestic workers, cooking, cleaning and caring, would be really surprised to know that 16 June has been declared as Domestic Workers Day by the International

Dinner with Manisha and Annapurna when Manisha came to Goa.

Labour Organization, or that the ILO has a Convention 189 on Decent Work for Domestic Workers. Each of these women sees herself as an individual struggling to survive in a harsh and cruel world. They would be shocked to know that there are 67.1 million domestic workers worldwide.

A recently published book called *Maid in India* by Tripti Lahiri (2017) reveals the staggering rise in the number of domestic workers in India. In the decade after liberalization, there was a nearly 120 percent rise: from 7.4 lakh in 1991 to 16.2 lakh workers by 2001. Women constitute over two-thirds of the workforce in this unorganized sector, which also includes chauffeurs and security guards. The domestic workers are beginning to be organized by the National Platform for Domestic Workers and in many towns and cities they have come together to observe 16 June; they are demanding minimum wages.

But this has not changed things much. The women who work in homes remain vulnerable to all kinds of exploitation and abuse. And so many of us do not even recognize how we are complicit in this exploitation.

~

I know that without these women Sebastian and I could not survive. But there are some days when we are by ourselves, and that's when Sebastian and I still experiment with cooking.

Sebastian had always wanted to learn to bake. He complained that most baking classes were for women only. On his sixty-sixth birthday I presented him with an old-fashioned oven, which he prefers to a microwave one.

I look for recipes on YouTube and then Sebastian bakes. Our most successful endeavour has been an orange cake with almond flour. It fills our house with the fragrance of oranges. And the cake is absolutely yummy.

~

I have been battling calories and cholesterol for many years; but I do not really have the motivation to go on a serious diet. I remember the old feminist classic *Fat is a Feminist Issue* by Susie Orback (1978). It was a pioneering anti-diet book. Orbach argued that gender inequality makes women fat. She wrote: 'For many women, compulsive eating and being fat have become one way to avoid being marketed or seen as the ideal woman. In other words, what your fat says about you is: "Screw you!" Fat expresses a rebellion against the powerlessness of the woman.'

In a report entitled 'Fat Activists Lash Out at Thinness Industry', I discovered that there are 'fat activists' fighting for a fat liberation movement. The news report said:

> Most fat-acceptance activists endorse the concept of eating healthy food and exercising regularly, but they oppose any fixation on losing weight and contend that more than 95 percent of diets fail. They also decry the rapid growth of stomach-shrinking surgery; the number of such procedures has quadrupled to 100,000 annually since 1998. Unashamed

> of their size, fed up with fat jokes, and angry at the national obsession with dieting, overweight activists are mounting a feisty protest movement against the medical establishment's campaign against obesity.

One day I felt there was a lump in my stomach. I went to see a doctor in Manipal hospital across the road from our apartment in Goa. The doctor felt my belly and said there was nothing wrong; but he sent me off to the biatric surgeon anyway. The biatric surgeon declared, without even examining me, that he would recommend a gastric sleeve surgery.

I sat opposite this young doctor and listened to him telling me what kind of surgery he was recommending. He glibly explained that the surgery was routine, nothing drastic at all. He drew a stomach on paper and showed me how much of my stomach he would cut and staple—and voila! I would be slim and healthy.

Susie Orbach never imagined her classic book would still be so relevant decades later. Writing in the *Guardian* in 2018, she said:

> The story of the past 40 years is grim. It's a story of malice, of greed and of mendacity. Not content with destabilising the eating of many western women and exporting body hatred all over the world as a sign of modernity, the combined forces of what investigative health reporter Alicia Mundy so aptly termed "Obesity Inc" set about to create new so-called disease entities; these would medicalise and pathologise people's relationship to food and their bodies so successfully that vast industries would grow up to treat problems that these industries had themselves instigated.

That day at the hospital in Goa, I looked at the doctor and knew him to be just a pawn in Obesity Inc; it would be a waste of my time to give him a piece of my feminist mind.

Sebastian and I went home and he roasted a chicken and mashed some potatoes. After that, I went on a diet and lost ten kilos because I wanted to. My motivation: we were going to Antarctica and I needed to fit into my new jacket bought at a store appropriately called 'Largely Yours'.

4

FLAVOURS OF CLASS, CASTE, RELIGION AND ETHNICITY

From the time that I was a child, I knew that there was a difference between the rich and the poor. However, I was not troubled because my parents assured me that in time the poor too would benefit from the rapid progress India was making. I had the impression that, with progress, the gap between the rich and the poor would close and slowly the poor would eventually have enough to eat, better housing, good education and medical facilities. I was brought up to believe that development would be the bridge which would close the gap between the rich and poor.

However, by the mid-1990s it was clear that with the kind of development policies India had chosen, the gap between the rich and the poor was in fact growing. The enormity of this gap was rarely written about in our popular press. P. Sainath, a journalist by profession and a former student of Jawaharlal Nehru University, observed that 'journalism has become the stenography of the powerful'. Sainath went around the poorest districts of India and documented the conditions of the people, and he published his reports in a book called *Everybody Loves a Good Drought*. The stories in the book first published in 1996 showed the horror behind the statistics: that 312 million Indian citizens lived below the poverty line, 26 million had been displaced by various development projects, and 13 million suffered from tuberculosis.

While *Everybody Loves a Good Drought* has become a classic, in media coverage the issues raised by Sainath still do not get the attention they deserve.

~

On 18 October 2017, even the mainstream media had to take notice of the grim reality of the lives of the Indian poor. The major dailies and electronic media told the story of an eleven-year-old girl, Santoshi Kumar, who died of starvation in a village in Jharkhand because the girl's family were denied the rations they were entitled to under the National Food Security Act, 2013. The family's ration card was cancelled because it had not been linked to an Aadhaar card. Under the law, such a denial is illegal. Besides, the girl's family claimed that they, in fact, had an Aadhaar card.

The Global Hunger Index 2017 proved the huge disconnect between India's relatively high levels of growth and its low ranks on human development.

The government which came to power with the slogan that it would ensure development for all responded to the news of the girl's death by sending a central team to investigate the matter. No one bothered to follow up with the enquiry. In a celebrity-driven culture, the media follows the personal relationships of Bollywood actors with more interest than the fate of those citizens who are denied their rights under the Constitution on a daily basis.

~

In the early 1980s, when I started my law practice in the Supreme Court, I thought I could help enforce the fundamental rights of the poor and make the Indian Constitution meaningful to their lives. It was a time when public interest litigation was being used to reach justice to the poor. I wanted to be a part of that process.

The people I represented in the court were invariably the poor—both urban and rural poor; they were bonded labourers, landless peasants and tribal peoples who had been deprived of their social, economic or political rights. Their cause was taken up by political organizations or human-rights groups fighting for the enforcement of fundamental rights with the help of public interest litigation cases.

One of the first cases I argued was a petition on behalf of the iron-ore miners in Chaibasa district in what was then Bihar, but now is in Jharkhand. One of the reliefs I asked for, and got, was clean drinking water for the workers in accordance with the Indian Contract Labour (Regulation and Abolition) Act, 1970. But the real question is, why should Indian citizens have to move the highest court of the land to get safe drinking water? Even more shocking was that the workers had to go on a ten-day strike to force the authorities to implement the Supreme Court's order.

Representing Adivasis in court also gave me an opportunity to see how they perceived cities like New Delhi. An activist from a village in Jharkhand had come to Delhi and I asked him how he liked the capital of India. Unfortunately, I do not remember his name but I still remember his reply. He said there were three things that had really surprised or shocked him: the first was that Delhi was like a jungle (he did not immediately see the irony of that statement); the second was that in Delhi one had to buy water to drink. He was referring to the trolleys that sold cold water in summer, for ten paise a glass back then. (This was before we started buying bottled water.) The third thing that left him wonderstruck was that dogs in Delhi travelled by car while he had to walk or take crowded buses.

Taking up cases on behalf of tribal people gave me glimpses of the conditions in which they live. But when I actually went to remote villages and met some of the poorest people living in our country, it was an altogether different experience. I clearly remember the faces of the tribal women I met deep in a forest in Kandhamal in Odisha in the mid-1980s. A young woman activist, Manju Dhal, had invited me to a meeting with these women. She wanted me to give a series of lectures on the Indian Constitution and the status of women. When I arrived, I found a gathering of Kui tribal women. All of them were very short; in fact, they seemed stunted by malnutrition. They were dependent on forest produce and for almost six months of the year they lived on jackfruit. They looked at me silently and when I tried to speak to them individually, I was told they did not know Hindi. My lecture would be translated into Oriya and then into Kui, their tribal language.

I stood before them, tall and well-fed and obviously well-off. The contrast between us was too much to bridge with rhetoric about women's rights. It was meaningless to say that all of us women suffered under a patriarchal system when the income gap stood like a massive chasm between us. I was not at all sure what I could say that could be meaningful. But they waited with expectation.

I decided that it might be useful to get their perspectives on the Indian Constitution. I told them that the Constitution of India gave all citizens, including each of them, certain rights. I would tell them these rights and then we could see how far the rights were relevant to their lives. We began with the right to equality before the law guaranteed under Article 14 of the Indian Constitution. Did we have equality?

The response was unanimous: 'NO!'

What kinds of inequality did they experience?

One of them said she felt angry that her son, whom she had brought up alone because her husband was a drunkard, was still known by that man's name and not as her son. Another woman said tribals and non-tribals were not treated the same, and there was great inequality between the rich and the poor people in the country.

Then I asked them to decide what rights they would include in the Constitution if they could have a say. And I remember two rights they wanted included: the right to sugar and the right to kerosene.

Kui women in Orissa

I remembered this experience when I was invited to speak on the occasion of International Women's Day at the Kalinga Institute of Social Sciences (KISS) at Bhubaneswar some thirty years later, in 2016. This is an institution founded as a tribal residential school in 1993 and run by a foundation. It now proudly claims to be the 'world's largest residential education institution for tribal children'.

Achyuta Samanta, the founder is a philanthropist and current member of parliament from the Biju Janata Dal. There were more than 25,000 tribal children studying at KISS when I visited it. It is completely free and fully residential, from kindergarten to post-graduation.

Achyuta Samanta, whom I found to be an unassuming man, summed up his own life's struggle in the following few lines in an interview he gave to a newspaper:

> I lost my father at the age of four. From that age I have been struggling. I struggled for food till the age of 25. And for the last 25 years I have been struggling to feed 25,000 poor children. At 50, my life is still a struggle. Bringing poor children from dense forests to a big city and giving them a decent life and education till the age of 25 requires a lot of courage. That is my contribution to society.

As I stood before the tribal children at KISS, I was remined of the Kui women and wondered whether any of these young ones could possibly be their grandchildren. And I wondered why the government had not been able to do what one man had achieved.

One teacher told me that one of the problems faced by the girls was the prevalence of child marriage and I should address the problem in my speech. Obviously, I could do nothing in one speech, so I taught the girls some of our slogans against dowry and forced marriage.

Recently, there has been some controversy about the curriculum followed at KISS and the role that the institution has played in the lives of the tribal people of Odisha. I have been troubled by this. For example, the International Union of Anthropological and Ethnological Sciences announced that it was withdrawing a plan to hold the next World Anthropology Congress, scheduled for 2023, at KISS in Bhubaneshwar. The Indian Anthropological Society, representing more than two thousand anthropologists, opposed the decision and issued a statement asking that KISS be reinstated as the host, but to no avail.

One of the criticisms of KISS is that it has done nothing to challenge the way society sees tribals as 'primitive' and 'backward'. But that is a criticism which applies to the work of most anthropologists, missionaries, administrators and academics from different disciplines; it is an attitude which certainly needs to be challenged. It should have been discussed at the anthropology congress and Achyuta Samanta should have been invited to speak and to listen. The boycott seemed to me just a show of muscle power and ordinary tribal people have once again become pawns in power politics.

Meanwhile, KISS has opened another school in Delhi and this time I have first-hand experience of the institution having admitted children of street performers whom no other school would admit. The education is free. The kids say they love the school and have been waiting for it to re-open after it had to be closed due to the COVID pandemic. One of the reasons they like the school, they say, is that they get good food to eat.

~

I got deeper insights into the callousness of government policies to food security after I met Shankar Guha Neogi (1943–1991), the legendary trade union leader based in Chhattisgarh. I met him when he came to Delhi for a human-rights meeting in 1977, if my memory is right; and then at our home when he came to thank Papa for helping to secure his release from jail.

It was because of my association with Neogi's Chhattisgarh Mukti Morcha (CMM) that I first heard of the late Dr R.H. Richharia, one of India's leading experts on rice. During his time as Director of the Madhya Pradesh Rice Research Institute, he collected an amazing 20,000 varieties of rice. Dr Richharia's career was however cut short, and he was treated very unfairly by the Government of India because he stood up to the International Rice Research Institute's machinations in the country. He exposed the role of transnational corporations in agribusiness which had all but destroyed India's rich bio-diversity. Dr Richharia demonstrated methods by which indigenous techniques could be improved to increase yields from local rice varieties by cloning. Shankar Guha Neogi and the CMM applied Dr Richharia's ideas and published a pamphlet based on his work, to inform farmers of the advantages of clonal propagation technique.

It was this association that first made me aware of the importance of biodiversity and how transnational corporations were stealing our seeds, killing our biodiversity. But it would be many more years before I really began to understand the true significance of these issues and how they relate to our food security.

~

The worst example of how cruel the state and the public can be to fellow citizens is the treatment meted out to the indigenous tribes living in the Andaman Islands. I went there in connection with a human-rights case in 1999; 36 Burmese freedom fighters had been betrayed by a rogue agent in the Indian military intelligence and had been in jail in Port Blair ever since.

I went to the Andaman Islands several times between 1999 and 2006 in connection with the case and later I wrote a book on the case entitled *Rogue Agent: How India's Military Intelligence Betrayed the Burmese Resistance* (2009). It was during that time I became aware of the five tribal groups consisting of the Great Andamanese, the Jarawa, the Onge, the Shompen and the Sentinelese. According to the 2011 census, there are only 44 Great Andamanese, 380 Jarawa, 101 Onge, 229 Shompen, and 15 Sentinelese remaining.

On one of my visits to the Andaman Islands, Sebastian and I decided to visit Maya Bunder, a settlement of Karen people. They were about to be deported to Myanmar, but I had got a stay order in time to stop the deportation. We thought it would be a good idea to go by taxi instead of taking the ship; it would give us mobility and we would travel through the thick rainforest.

We booked a taxi and the driver was a local. By that I mean he was a descendent of the prisoners sent to the Andaman Islands by the British. They formed a distinct community with members who were Hindus and Muslims and spoke a distinct language, which was a wonderful mixture of many languages such as Punjabi, Urdu, Pashto and I do not know what else. Just before we started the journey, the driver went to a shop and bought a massive bunch of bananas. We protested that we did not want to eat bananas. He informed us that he had bought them for the members of the Jarawa community whom we would encounter in the jungles.

Before we entered the jungle there was a forest checkpoint where we stopped. The driver went to get the requisite permit, leaving us to read the Forest Department's red-and-green noticeboard:

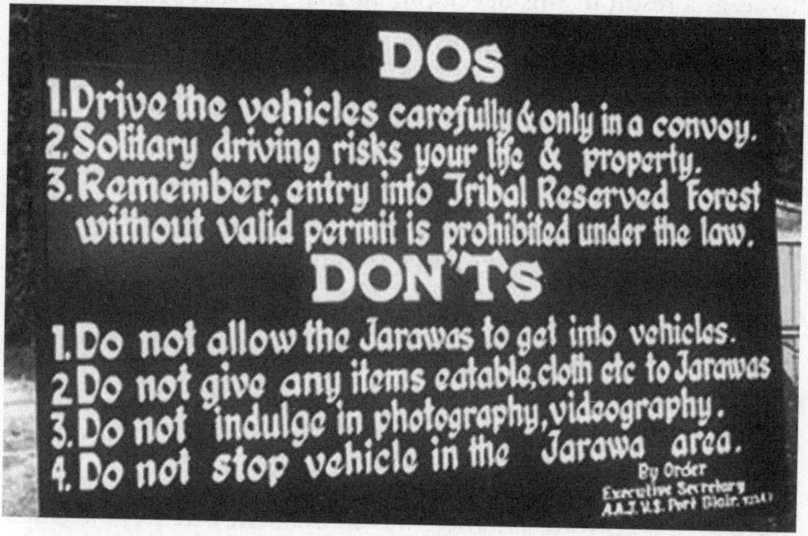

Our driver returned. By this time we were both feeling very uncomfortable. I could see that Sebastian felt a sense of identity and solidarity with the Jarawa. As we drove deep into the emerald-green forest the driver suddenly stopped and excitedly pointed out a Jarawa man walking with his little son. They were not at all self-conscious about the fact that they wore no clothes.

The driver stopped so that we could look at the man, but we kept telling him that we did not want to indulge in this obscene voyeurism. The driver could not understand our reaction and handed some bananas to the Jarawa man, who took them with a smile.

Sebastian and the Jarawa man smiled at each other for a brief moment and we drove on. The driver asked whether we would like to see how the Jarawa lived and he could not understand why we said 'no' so vehemently.

At the time we did not realize we were driving down the Great Andaman Trunk Road, which has been the centre of controversy. It was as a result of this development that disease spread into the Jarawa community and many had died in a measles epidemic.

Poachers, too, have been responsible for introducing alien and harmful products like alcohol to the tribe, and forest officers take presents of food, such as cake and biscuits, which has affected the traditional way of life of the Jarawa who live by hunting and gathering. Now the younger members of the community wait by the road and ask for food instead of hunting.

The road makes it easier for tourists to go into the forests. It is estimated that some five hundred tourists a day are taken through the forest to stare at the tribals; and they invariably take 'gifts' of food such as bananas for the people to lure them into coming to the road to be gawked at. There was an incident when a policeman was bribed to allow a tourist to dance with a Jarawa woman.

~

I did not associate poverty and famines with the Northeast region. So when I first learnt that the roots of the Mizo insurgency lay in the famine of 1958-59, I was shocked.

Normally, the bamboo is a symbol of long life and good fortune. But once in every twenty-five years, the bamboo blooms and fruits. This attracts millions of rats. The rats first feast on the bamboo flowers and fruits. When they have finished, they turn to the crops and within a day or two all the crops are devoured. And people are faced with famine. It is called the bamboo death.

The short famine is called 'thingtam' and the long famine is called 'mautam' or bamboo death. The history of Mizoram, in a way, begins with mautam when the bamboo flowered in 1958, and there was a terrible famine in the Mizo Hills, then a part of Assam. The famine pushed the Mizos into the jungles for survival. They had to leave their homes in search of food and lived on roots and leaves, but many died of starvation. Neither the Government of Assam nor the Government of India responded to the anguish of the Mizo people. They did not send any relief and the entire country was totally ignorant of the sufferings of their fellow citizens.

Mizos have always relied on their own strength and resilience as a community. In 1958, many Mizos raised money and organized relief for their own people. Among them was Pu Laldenga, a clerk in a bank and the secretary of the Mizo Cultural Society. He converted the cultural society into the 'Mautam Front' and very efficiently organized famine relief in the rural areas. By March 1960, the Front had renamed itself as the Mizo National Famine Front.

Adding insult to injury, the Assam Government tried to impose the Assamese language on Mizos and other ethnic groups by making it the only official language of the state. The Mizo National Famine Front soon dropped the 'Famine' from its name and converted itself into a political organization. The MNF was born on 22 October 1961. It began by demanding the unification of all the Mizo areas in Assam, Manipur and Tripura under one administration. When there was no response to their demands, the MNF launched their movement for an independent, sovereign Mizoram.

The armed insurrection began on 28 February 1966 with attacks on the government installations at Aizawl, Lunglei, Chawngte, Chhimluang and other places. And on 1 March 1966, Laldenga declared independence for Mizoram.

During the counter-insurgency operations, the Indian security forces uprooted people from 516 villages and put them into concentration camps. This meant that 80 percent of the population of the Mizo Hills was made homeless. Officially, this was called regrouping of people in 'protected and progressive' villages.

On 5 and 6 March 1966, the Government of India bombed the city of Aizawl with Toofani and Hunter jet fighters. Among the pilots was Squadron Leader Rajeshwar Prasad Singh Bidhuri, better known as the politician Rajesh Pilot. This was the first time India used her Air Force to quell a movement of any kind among her citizens. Hundreds of bombs reduced houses, schools, markets, churches and even hospitals to ash. Miraculously, only fifteen people died in Aizawl, but that was because most of the 10,000-odd residents of the hill town had fled when fighting between the Mizo nationalists and Indian security forces began.

Many people still remember the terrifying sight of planes and of bombs exploding in huge balls of fire and devastating their neighbourhood. Mizo historians have preserved the shells that were dropped at that time and have documented the events of those days.

The Prime Minister at the time told the Indian Parliament that the planes had dropped only food packets. Ironically, it was the Assam government that exposed the lie. It sent a fact-finding mission consisting of three members, all of whom were Khasis from the Khasi Hills district (which later became Meghalaya): Stanley D.D. Nichols Roy, Hoover H. Hynniewta, and Lok Sabha MP from Shillong, G.G. Swell. The team collected a lot of evidence about the bombings and their report is part of the Assam Assembly proceedings.

Finally, after two decades of resistance, the Government of India and the Mizo National Front negotiated a settlement called the Mizo Accord. The Accord was signed on 30 June 1986. On

20 February 1987, at a public meeting at Aizawl, a proclamation announced that Mizoram would be declared a full-fledged state of India. Pu Laldenga became the first chief minister.

If you go to Mizoram they will show you a place called 'Laldenga London'. These are the caves in which the Mizo leader hid when the Indian Government thought he was in London.

~

Even when the communities living in the Northeast did not suffer famine or drought, they had to face severe shortage of salt. There are accounts of how fiercely the Nagas had to guard their precious salt wells from the Ahom kings. The shortage of salt meant that the Nagas and other communities living in the Northeast had to find substitutes for salt; the substitute is called khar. In Assam khar was made from filtering water through the ashes of sundried banana peels. This is just one of the many ingenious recipes for khar.

~

In the past, the man (yes, not the woman) who was accorded the highest status in Naga society was the one who owned the biggest store of grains and the largest herd of cattle—but he would earn the respect of society only *after* he had given it all away. He had to give away his entire wealth in a series of feasts of merit to the village. It could be up to thirty feasts. After that, he and his wife were given the honour of erecting a special kind of pole, or the right to wear certain kinds of ornaments or a special shawl.

One of my most prized possessions is a plain white shawl given to me by the villagers of Oinam in the Senapati district of Manipur. They gave me the Feast of Merit shawl in 1991 at the end of my four-year-long court battle against the Indian armed forces for committing human-rights violations during a counter-insurgency operation in 1987 codenamed Operation Bluebird.

The final hearing before the Gauhati High Court was over in 1991. We all waited for the Judgement. But when the High Court did not give its judgement for 25 years, Sebastian and I wrote a book entitled *The Judgement That Never Came: Army Rule in Northeast India* (2011).

The Judgement was finally delivered in 2019. The judges stated that they could not give a proper judgement because the files were incomplete. No one bothered to ask how the files had got lost. There would be no justice for the victims of Operation Bluebird; and I would never wear the Feast of Merit shawl. It still lies at the bottom of my suitcase, a constant reminder of the great injustice to the people who had put their faith in the Indian courts.

~

Nagas say they eat everything that flies, except airplanes; and everything that walks, except human beings. The Naga diet consisted traditionally of a large number of green leaves and many different kinds of vegetables, roots and herbs; and they had access to a large variety of non-vegetarian food such as snails, frogs, insects, fish, beef, chicken and everyone's favourite was and is, of course, pork.

I saw first-hand how the diet of the Nagas has depleted over the years. In part, this is because of the negative impact on the biodiversity by the kind of developmental projects being undertaken. I understood how development could have adverse effects on the diet of tribal people when I took up the case of the Hundung villagers living in the Ukhrul district of Manipur.

In the 1970s, the Centre set up the North East Council, a statutory authority charged with the duty to ensure balanced development of the region. One of its first projects was to set up a cement factory in Hundung village. On 6 January 1981, the

Government of Manipur brought out a Notification announcing that the compensation for villagers who would lose their land would be 0.04 paise per square foot for second-grade land and 0.06 paise for first-grade land. The villagers challenged this Notification, but they lost the case at the lower level because, they said, they could not afford to pay a bribe to the judge.

The case went up to the High Court but nothing came of it. In 1988, I was in Manipur in connection with the Oinam case. At that time friends from Hundung asked me to take up their case. The villagers had formed themselves into a group called the Victims of Development. I filed a public interest litigation case in 1990. One of the aspects of the case was the loss of paddy fields, kitchen gardens and forest-land—all of which affected the diet of the villagers. The land taken away for the cement factory and the mini hydro-electricity project included their prized wet paddy fields. In fact, their paddy fields were the best in the entire district. Since the construction of the Nungshangkong Mini Hydro Electricity project, the water had been diverted to the cement factory, thus converting the wet paddy fields into dry fields.

In the wet paddy field, the cultivators have fishponds and its fertility allows for inter-cropping of maize, beans, soya beans, etc. Thus the yield of the wet paddy field is 80 percent higher than a dry paddy field. A wet paddy field not only yields more paddy than a dry field, but is also a source of fish, frogs and a variety of insects which are eaten and are a cheap source of proteins. I sat with the villagers and made an elaborate chart of the number of fish, insects and snails available in a wet paddy field, and their value in calories, and translated that into monetary terms. The person who helped me to understand the ecology of the wet paddy field was Dr Ngachan Francis, an agricultural scientist who was working in the Indian Council of Agricultural Research (ICAR); he was from Hundung.

The villagers had been hesitant to talk about the things they ate because they knew that in the eyes of the non-tribals, their food was not civilized and they felt embarrassed to say they ate snails, frogs and insects. But gradually they overcame their hesitation. When we had finally completed the chart and calculated the total value in calories, they realized just how much they had lost.

I submitted the chart in court as evidence of the extent of loss and demanded compensation on the basis of this. Luckily, two Naga judges, Justice Sema and Justice Shishak, heard the case and accepted our contention, and the villagers won their case, including compensation for the loss in their diet.

The case came up in the Supreme Court where the judges commented on the unusual way of calculation for compensation but accepted it. If you read the Order in State of Manipur and Another vs Humdung Victims of Development given on 6 December 1994 (equivalent citations: AIR 1995 SC 1875), it only states 'Compensation for loss of pisciculture and also loss of yield of paddy', and has no reference to our elaborate chart.

The two Naga judges were never again put on the same Bench again.

~

While I was working on the case, I spent a night at Hundung village. That night, there was a great deal of excitement because the villagers were going to smoke out the wasps and get the hive. This was the first time I saw such a massive hive—three- or four-storeys high, it had formed underground and was stuck to a rock.

When the wasp hive was brought to the kitchen of the owner of the hive, children gathered around. I saw one of them steal a larva and pop it into his mouth. The elders sat with the kids and explained all about the wasps and how they turn from the egg to larvae and then spin themselves into cocoons and finally emerge as wasps or bees.

I remembered how Amma, a trained school teacher, had caught caterpillars and put them in tea tins so I could see how a caterpillar turned into a beautiful butterfly. Except that each time she did it, our caterpillars turned into moths—but it had been exciting to watch nature at work!

~

Talking of bees and wasps, there is another story which shows the difference in the attitude to bees between Nagas and mainlanders living in the city.

The Naga insurgent group, the National Socialist Council of Nagalim (NSCN-IM), and the Government of India began peace talks in 1997. Deepak Dewan, a journalist working with the Delhi-based weekly, *The North East Sun*, had a role in initiating the talks. On one occasion, the NSCN leaders and Indian officials met at his home. His mother brought in the tea and some snacks. When the meeting was over, she told her son that she had been really struck by the courage of the Nagas.

Deepak asked his mother how she had come to this conclusion after seeing them sitting in the drawing room. She said she had seen a bee buzzing around the room and had been afraid it would sting someone. Just then one of the Nagas had simply caught it in his hand and held it in his fist without interrupting the conversation.

~

When Nagas come to work in towns and cities as migrant workers, they are faced with great hardships and prejudices. Many of them cannot afford to buy meat or even vegetables.

While we were studying in Jawaharlal Nehru University there was a student who was known for catching peacocks and eating them. He told me he had caught ninety-nine peacocks, so I asked why he had not made it to a century. He said that just before he could reach that number, he got into the civil services and naturally had to give up eating the national bird.

I remembered him when some students phoned me sometime in July of 2011 to say a migrant worker, Chinaugam, had been arrested in Gurgaon and was lodged in jail for killing two peacocks. That was when I saw the post mortem of a peacock for the first and only time in my life.

Dr Rajesh Godara was the veterinary surgeon who conducted the post mortem and he told the court during the trial: 'In my opinion the death may be due to injury by blunt object and compressing the neck which leads to death due to asphyxia. The birds were male peacocks and unfeathered (sic). Post mortem was conducted in the hospital and after conducting postmortem the dead bodies of birds were handed over to the police.'

The trial was all about the murder of two peacocks by a human being; the accused was treated by the police, the courts and the bar as an inferior species because he ate peacocks. No one was concerned with the facts and circumstances of why he had to take the risk of breaking the law—he had no job and no other means of feeding himself and his family.

We finally did get Chinaugam out on bail with the help of a Naga IAS officer. However, the last time I checked, while writing this book, the case was still pending in the courts, so Chinaugam continues to live in fear of being picked up again and convicted.

~

Desperate for their own cuisines, migrant workers from the Northeast living in cities and towns across India have started opening their own restaurants which serve their home food at reasonable rates. Some enterprising men and women living in Mumbai, Bengaluru and Delhi have started to import fresh vegetables flown directly from Manipur by cargo. And almost all of them manage to grow some essentials in pots on their balconies.

In Goa, we have a restaurant called Meiphung Oriental which serves delicacies from the Northeast and attracts not only residents and visitors from that region but has also won fans among Indian and foreign tourists. Goans, too, have started enjoying a Naga pork curry and fried beef salad or a spicy Umrok chutney. The owner of the restaurant, Livingstone Shaiza, told me recently that a Goan guest has deposited Rs 15,000 with him and orders food on the phone. Shaiza delivers the food as a special case.[19] Sebastian and I also enjoy the smoked pork and rice wine at Meiphung.

~

The very first time I tasted a Naga pork curry, I fell in love with their food. As time passed, I learnt that there was not just one kind of pork curry. The meat has very different kinds of taste, depending on whether it has been smoked on the fireplace or kept with the paddy till it ferments.

There are many ways in which the Nagas cook pork; it can be cooked with a variety of herbs and spices, such as bamboo shoots, sesame seeds, smoked chillies, fermented soya beans, and sometimes it can be combined with special vegetables such as the roots of a squash. Traditionally, the pork was not fried but plain boiled with salt and chillies, and then the herbs and vegetables were added.

Cooking pork for a feast in Ukhrul.

I remember Sebastian had cooked a pork curry with rice and a chutney for Alice Thorner (1917–2005), an old family friend of ours, and her friend Violette Graff, a French anthropologist. They came to our home in Bangalore where I was teaching the first course on human rights at the National Law School (NLSUI). Violette loved the food, but it was the chutney that she liked most of all. She said it was just like the French chicken liver pâté. This made me realize just how sophisticated Naga cuisine is.

In Europe, they flavour the chicken liver pâté with alcohol: Madeira, port, cognac or brandy. But I agree with Violette that the Naga chicken liver chutney can rival the rich, silky French delicacy. And it is easy to make.

NAGA CHICKEN LIVER CHUTNEY

Ingredients

- The liver of one chicken
- 2 pods of garlic

- 1 Umrok (Naga King Chilly) or smoked red chillies
- Salt

Method

- Boil the chicken liver with the garlic till it is soft. If you prefer a stronger garlic taste then crush it raw. The chilly can be either roasted on the flame or boiled. Mix all the ingredients into a smooth paste, adding a little of the water in which the liver was boiled. The chicken liver chutney is ready!

~

There is no occasion which is not celebrated with pork—that is if a Naga family can afford it. This is something the tribal communities share with the Dalits. However, since Dalits live in close proximity to upper-caste Hindus, their reactions to pork eating can be quite different, as I found from reading Sujatha Gidla's memoirs, *Ants among Elephants: An Untouchable Family and the Making of Modern India* (2017). Gidla describes the reaction of her brother, a Dalit and a Naxalite leader, to pork on the eve of his wedding:

> Satyam considered it uncultured and even barbaric to eat the flesh of a pig on any occasion. A pig, to caste Hindus, is a symbol of filth. Untouchables are commonly associated with two creatures: the crow for its blackness and the pig for its foulness. When people assembled under the banyan tree to plan the feast, Satyam told them there would be no pig.
>
> The elders took the cigars out of their mouths. 'What, what! A wedding feast with no pig?'
>
> Satyam replied, 'There won't be any meat.'

I read this out to Sebastian and he said: 'Why should we cater to upper-caste tastes?' I liked the 'we', but the realities of tribal communities and Dalits are of course far apart.

~

The thing that takes time to get used to is the smell of some of the favourite fermented foods in the Northeast. I remember our Tamil neighbours living in the flat above us were repulsed by the smell of ngari wafting up to their home. The husband came to beg us not to cook whatever it was that we were cooking because it was making his wife vomit.

Ngari is prepared by fermenting small freshwater fish with mustard oil and salt. The dried fish are then tightly packed into airtight clay urns. The urn is then buried for 30 to 40 days. Ngari is added to various dishes in Manipuri cuisine, especially the famous Eromba. The word 'Eromba' is derived from 'eeru taana lonba' in Manipuri which means 'mixing, stirring, watery'. The dish is usually made with boiled vegetables and fermented fish mashed together along with chillies. A touch of fermented bamboo gives it an extra flavour.

~

The special flavours in Naga cuisine and in the cuisines of the Northeast come from the fermentation of food which gives it an umami taste. This is the fifth taste, which has been officially recognized in addition to salty, sweet, sour and bitter. Umami is a loan word from the Japanese and may be translated as 'pleasant savory taste'. This neologism was coined in 1908 by Japanese chemist Kikunae Ikeda from a word meaning 'delicious'.

Scientists have debated whether umami is a basic taste ever since Kikunae Ikeda first proposed its existence in 1908. In 1985, umami was recognized as the scientific term to describe the taste of glutamates and nucleotides at the first Umami International Symposium in Hawaii. It can be described as a pleasant 'brothy' or 'meaty' mouth-watering taste which lingers for a long time.

There are many fermented preparations which enhance Naga

cuisine. Ashiho A. Mao and N. Odyuo have described these in an article published in the *Journal of Traditional Knowledge* (Volume 6 (1) January 2007, pp. 37–41).

> The first is anishi. Anishi is prepared from the leaf of the edible Colocasia species mainly by the Ao Naga tribe. The fresh mature green leaves are taken, washed, and then the leaves are staked one above the other and finally wrapped with banana leaf. They are then kept aside for about a week till the leaves turn yellow. The yellow leaves are then ground into paste and cakes are made out of it. The cakes are dried over the fireplace in the kitchen. During grinding if desired, chilli, salt and ginger are added to it. The dried cakes are ready for use; they are cooked with dry meat, especially pork, which is the favourite dish of the Ao tribe.

I still remember when I first tasted anishi. To me it tasted just like Marmite—the spread made from yeast extract which in British popular culture is often used as a metaphor for something that is an acquired taste or tends to polarise opinion. Marmite is particularly rich in umami due to its very high levels of glutama.

Then there is axone (akhone), fermented soya bean, which is popular among the Sema Nagas. It is prepared by boiling the beans till they become soft. The water is drained out and the cooked beans are then wrapped in banana leaves and kept above the fireplace to ferment for a week. The beans are ready to be used in chutney preparations along with chilli, tomato and salt. However, for long-term storage and depending on choice of taste, the fermented beans are kept in cake form above the fireplace, or individual beans are separated, dried in the sun and stored in containers. The dried beans or cakes are cooked with pork or are used for the preparation of chutneys.

In 2019 a Hindi film was released called Axone, made by

Nicholas Kharkongor. Axone is a metaphor for the division that exists between the people of the Northeast and the rest of India. It is a comedy drama about a group of Northeast migrant workers in Delhi trying to find a place where they can cook a dish with axone or akhoni for a wedding feast.

~

I have attempted to appreciate all aspects of Naga cuisine and have tried a large variety of dishes. But there was one time I failed to live up to my host's expectations. This was when I was in Patkai Christian College in Dimapur. I had spent the night at the home of our friend Tuimatai Shimray. In the morning he picked up two juicy silkworms and asked which one I would like for my breakfast. I had shared the room the previous night with a lot of silkworms crawling all over the fresh green leaves spread over much of the floor. I did not dare go to the toilet for fear of stepping on the silkworms. So when Shimray asked about breakfast, I chickened out and had an egg and toast instead. Amma would not have been pleased with my cowardice.

~

By the time a Naga child is eight or nine, he or she is already a useful member of the community and has learnt skills of survival; the children can provide for themselves if necessary. They know about the basics of gardening, how to hunt small animals and distinguish between edible and poisonous fruits. The contrast between the knowledge of a Naga child and a child raised in the cities was brought home to me when I returned to Delhi after my mother died in November 1989.

I was exhausted and had very low blood pressure. I was lying on the carpet in my father's home, unable to get up. It was afternoon and the only person in the room was my nephew, Ashwin Mushran, the grandson of my father's sister, Saraswati. He had just passed out from Doon School. His mother Linnet, famed for her Bhuira jams, was very proud of the 10,000-word essay her son had written on Tolkien's *Lord of the Rings*.

I called out to Ashwin to make me a cup of coffee. He came to the room looking rather shamefaced and said he had never made any before. I told him to go into the kitchen and I shouted out instructions. He did finally produce a cup of coffee. When his mother heard of his achievement, she told everyone.

Soon after, I left for Guwahati to continue the case I was working on. I was going to stay with a Naga friend, Asholi Mao, in the Mission Compound of the Council of Baptist Churches of North East India (CBCNEI). Asholi was not at home but his ten-year-old nephew, Adani, saw me and quickly took my bag and carried it to the house. He had made the bed and offered to cook lunch. By the time I finished washing up, the little boy had made rice and curry for me. I asked what the curry was. He said he had taken his catapult and shot a bird outside and cleaned and cooked it.

Adani's skills in survival, his ability to look after himself and me, are not respected as knowledge in our society. But what should be more valued: an ability to write an essay on Tolkien or the ability to survive and to look after yourself and others? Or, perhaps, both?

Some time ago, I was visiting the home of my cousin, Dipak Haksar. Sebastian and I were sitting in his drawing room having tea. His mother, my Chachi, was also present, as were his wife and her mother, and Dipak's daughter. Archana, Dipak's wife, was feeding their Tibetan dog from a bowl with a spoon. (Sebastian, thankfully, refrained from commenting on that. I knew he felt dogs should not be treated as children.) At one point, Dipak reminded me of the first time he had cooked chicken in my parent's home in Delhi. He was in his twenties then, and had recently learnt how to cut and clean a chicken during a stint in the kitchen of the Maurya Hotel as a part of his management training.

'Didda, do you remember how the Nagas made fun of me?' he asked.

Indeed, I did. Some of my Naga friends were visiting and saw Dipak chop off the head of the chicken and drop it into a large bowl for discards. Then he chopped off the legs and threw them into the bowl. Then he scooped out the liver… At this point, one of the Nagas, Samuel, protested. 'He's throwing away the best parts!'

I told my friends to refrain from making Dipak self-conscious. But after he had finished cooking his chicken the Nagas retrieved all the parts he had thrown away and cooked a proper curry, Naga style.

There was shocked silence in the drawing room when I recalled this incident. Finally, Chachi broke the silence. 'Apne, apne taste hote hain (Different people have different tastes),' she said, trying to sound reasonable and conciliatory. Clearly no one wanted to offend Sebastian by saying what they really thought—that Naga tastes were inferior to those of the cultured lot who dined at exclusive hotels.

~

It is not only tribal cuisine that is denigrated, but also the food that the urban poor sell. I saw this when the Bombay (as it was then) Municipal Corporation tried to chase away street vendors by whipping up fear that street food causes stomach upsets.

We often think that the food made by poor people is dirty and that the food served in five-star hotels is more hygienic. I am also guilty of this perception. So, when the sugarcane juice-walas were being evicted in Bombay I did not pay much attention. I was in the city working with Indira Jaisingh's Lawyers Collective at the time. The Bombay Municipal Corporation had put out advertisements in the front pages of the newspapers warning people that they would get stomach trouble if they drank sugarcane juice from street vendors; they said it had a high *E. coli* content.

Anand Grover, Indira's husband and also a lawyer, was trained in chemistry and decided to challenge this finding. He took samples of the sugarcane juice as well as samples of milk shakes from two five-star hotels and a hotel owned by the then Mayor of Bombay. The samples were sent to laboratories and the results showed that the milk shakes had a much higher E. coli content.

This was in part the basis of how Indira Jaisingh won the right of Bombay hawkers to hawking zones. But the Supreme Court judgment of 1985 was not implemented for more than twenty years, even though street vending is an important form of self-employment for the poor in India. Hawkers play a vital role in the economy: (1) they distribute items of daily consumption at relatively low prices to all classes of consumers at convenient locations; and (2) they help the farm sector as well as small-scale industry, by acting as channels of distribution of their goods in every nook and corner of the country at minimal costs, bringing vitality to the urban economy.

The government estimates that India has ten million street vendors (including those who sell vegetables or street food), and their combined turnover is at least Rs 86,000 crores. After a long struggle, the street vendors organized themselves, and now lakhs are members of the National Association of Street Vendors of India

(NASVI), which was formed in 1998. The Association was at the forefront in the fight to have a law to protect street vendors, and in 2014 the Indian Parliament finally passed the Street Vendors (Protection of Livelihood and Regulation of Street Vending) Act. But the provisions of the law have not given adequate protection to the street vendors and during the COVID pandemic they were badly hit.

~

Once, when Sebastian and I were in Guwahti in connection with a human-rights case in the late 1980s, I told him that I wanted to eat at Woodlands in Dispur. At that time there were very few restaurants in Guwahati and even fewer in Imphal. We had a nice big crisp masala dosa and I remarked: 'It is nice to have home food.'

Sebastian could not understand how I could call a dosa 'home food'. But for me it was as familiar and comforting as a Kashmiri meal. Almost every Sunday we used to get our lunch from Karnataka Bhavan, opposite my parents' home in Delhi. But then Sebastian, too, enjoys his idlis every Sunday, which he goes to buy at Kamat in Panaji; it's just that he does not call it 'home' food.

I know that when Indians go abroad the thing they miss most is Indian food. I remember my conversations with my friend Abdul Majid of the Institute of Economic Growth in Delhi. One day, he and I, along with another friend, were sitting in the garden of a restaurant in Delhi enjoying the winter sun. The conversation centred on kebabs. They enthusiastically discussed the taste, textures and origins of a variety of kebabs: shammi, gulati, sheekh, kacche-keema ke kebab and so many other varieties I had never heard of. The animated mouth-watering discussion was entirely in Urdu, which lent it a literary air.

By the end of an hour I was hungry. Majid Sahib called the waiter and asked what kinds of kebabs they had on the menu. The waiter replied: 'We only have hamburgers, Sahib.' Both my friends sighed and shook their heads.

Many years later, Majid Sahib had retired and shifted from his home in Old Delhi to Gurgaon. He took me to his rooftop. He had made a beautiful garden where he had cages for his beloved pigeons. They were beautiful; white, grey and black. Majid Sahib said they were trained but had got totally disoriented after coming to Gurgaon. I asked him how his son was doing in America. He said his son had decided to return to India. I asked why, especially as he had a Green Card. Majid Sahib replied: 'He says he misses the kebabs.'

I knew Majid Sahib made a joke of serious things and hid his pain behind humour and Urdu poetry. I wondered what the real reason for his son's return was. Could it really just be the food?

~

Is there an Indian culture, an Indian cuisine or an Indian ethos? Each community in India is fiercely proud of its food and thinks it is the best. This is something I have encountered in my everyday interactions.

Once I was invited to lunch by Bhagirathi, a friend from Karnataka. She had passed out of the National School of Drama; while studying there she had met Bahrul Islam and they got married and moved to Guwahati. Bhagirathi said it had been very difficult to adjust to Assam, especially since she did know the language. Then with her usual grit and determination she learnt Assamese and even won a special prize for her role in an Assamese film. But she missed her food. She had made fish for me:

Bhagirathi and Bahrul.

one cooked in the Assamese style and the other in her 'home' style. She invited me to taste both and judge which was better. That was not an invitation I accepted and insisted that both were equally good!

Bhagirathi belongs to a Marathi-speaking community living in Karnataka. She said once when she made rotis with salt her mother had scolded her. Did she not know that in their community they never put salt in rotis? I asked her why and she said that it was from the time of Shivaji. Since salt made you thirsty, Shivaji, the hardy 'warrior', did not have salt in his rotis. And this had become an unalterable tradition among all Marathas, regardless of their profession and living conditions.

As I have reiterated several times, my parents had brought me up as an Indian and instilled the fact that we were Indian first, Indian second and Indian last. It took me a long time to understand that however deeply an average Indian may be committed to his or her country, each one is equally, perhaps even more strongly, committed to his or her regional identity, especially its culture and cuisine. Not surprisingly, when Indians have conflicts among themselves they make fun of or denigrate each other's food. This is based on ignorance and plain prejudice.

One such divide is between the rice- and roti-eating people. During the Assam agitation I remember someone saying that the definition of an Indian from mainstream India was a chapatti-eating, Hindi-speaking person.

~

Raju, the namkeenwala who has been coming to our home for donkey's years, is a Gujarati-speaking roti-eating Indian. He used to come to our home when my parents were alive and he continues to visit Sebastian and me whenever we are in Delhi. He arrives with two sturdy canvas bags packed with savouries from Gujarat, including khakhra, mixtures made of flattened rice mixed with peanuts, large, thick potato chips coated with red chilli powder, sweet lemon pickle without any oil and, if we are lucky, freshly made khandavi.

Raju lives across the Jamuna river and cycles all over south Delhi, going house-to-house selling his wares. He is always polite and smiling, ready to have a conversation or to just sell and leave if you look busy. In the old days, much of the things he brought were made by his wife and sister-in-law, but over the years he has also been bringing packaged foods. He would tell us he had made enough to build a small house back in Gujarat and he was dreaming of going back.

Then on 26 January 2001 an earthquake struck Gujarat. His newly built house was one of the 400,000 homes that were destroyed. Luckily, no one from his family died in the quake. Now he had to support his homeless parents and start saving to build another house. The assistance package of one billion US dollars did not help him. The only thing he ever complained to me about was that he did not have a television so he could relax in the evenings.

Raju cycled in the heat or cold, covering more than 25 to 30 kilometres every day. His only grouse was that many Residents Welfare Associations had stopped allowing vendors like him into their colonies, and some took money for permission to do so. He was really quite excited that his friend had invited him to Goa for a contract job. He hoped to make good money. We gave him our address in Goa and invited him to our home.

One day, Sebastian found Raju sitting in the teashop right below our house. We were all excited to meet and had a good tea together. Raju said his job was to provide Gujarati food to the construction workers employed at the Manipal Hospital across the road. The workers could not bear to eat the local food which was mostly fish and rice; they wanted their rotis and sabzi.

But after some time Raju decided to return to Delhi. The friend who had brought him to Goa had cheated him; he hadn't given Raju the amount that was promised. But he was an old friend and Raju let it go. So would he be coming back to Goa, I asked. 'No,' he said. 'I don't like the food. I can't get used to eating rice every day.'

This was also a lesson that ordinary Indians love their regional cuisine as much as they love their country. Why should anyone have to choose between love of their region and their country? Why can't they have two or three identities and still claim India as the place to which they belong?

~

Rice-eaters are no less committed to their carbs; and it is not only Indian rice-eaters but also our Burmese neighbours. During the 1990s I worked to get several Burmese student activists released from jail in Imphal. They had taken shelter in India from the brutal military rule in their country, but when they arrived, they found themselves in democratic India's prisons for not having valid travel documents.

Having got the bail order for the Burmese, Sebastian and I were back in Guwahati. Early one morning, the doorbell rang and Sebastian opened the door to find the eight Burmese students, smiling.

I was in the midst of drafting the final arguments and I did not want to cope with cooking and looking after guests, so I told Sebastian to take the men to the local gurudwara, which was walking distance from our place. I thought of this idea because when I was practicing in the Supreme Court, many times my clients would go to the gurudwara where they got free food at the langar and free accommodation for three days. But Sebastian was bewildered by my directions.

'Gurudwara, what is that?' 'A Sikh temple.'

'I have never been into a Sikh temple.' 'There is always a first time.'

I did not really explain much, just told Sebastian to take the Burmese there. He came back really pleased. The gurudwara had welcomed them and given them a clean place to sleep and offered free food. They were not asked to which religion they belonged or why they were taking refuge in the temple. I went back to my work peacefully, relieved.

Soon enough there was another ring at the door. Sebastian announced that the Burmese had returned. They said the gurudwara only served rotis and they would much rather cook rice and curry in our kitchen!

The food served in the langars of gurudwaras is very good; and it is distributed to anyone who goes there. The food is cooked and served by volunteers who perform this duty every single day. It is presented without distinction of faith, religion, background or caste. And it is free.

I was shocked, therefore, to learn that there are special gurudwaras for Dalit Sikhs. The caste system has crept into every religion in India.

~

I am aware of how deeply ignorant I am about all matters relating to caste. In a way, my understanding of the caste system began with my interactions with the Burmese refugees, most of whom were Buddhists of the Theravada school. I adopted several of them and they became a part of our family.

I remember when Shar, a student from Mandalay University, came to my parents' home the first time. He served himself the rice and vegetables but he kept taking the dal straight from the serving bowl, taking sips repeatedly from the serving spoon. I tried to give him the dal in a katori but he smiled and said, 'In Burma we all eat from the same bowl.'

Shar's farewell party.

In many cultures people regularly eat from a common plate; the Nagas used to have common wooden plates, and eating from the same plate has always been one of the most common dietary social customs in Ethiopia, as it is among many Muslim communities in India and abroad. It is primarily the upper-caste Hindus with their inherently discriminatory and absurd notion of purity—and other groups who now emulate them in order to claim superiority over those 'below' them—who do not share a plate of food even among the best of friends or in the same family.

Even in liberal Hindu homes like mine when I was young, we would find it difficult to share a plate of food with our guests.

~

There were many other lessons I learnt from the Burmese Buddhists. Soe Myint, a student from Rangoon University, told me that he was taking pork for a Buddhist monk living in Bodh Gaya. I was horrified. I said it was not good to break religious tenets; it was disrespectful. Soe was surprised and said, 'But Aunty, Buddhism does not forbid eating of meat.'

I could not believe what I was hearing. I thought vegetarianism in India was the result of Buddhist influence. But after my interaction with the Burmese Buddhists I realized that I needed to re-think the whole question of the origins of vegetarianism.

I remembered a book given to me long ago by Bhagwan Das (1927–2010), a lawyer whom I met in the Supreme Court. He was a Buddhist and a follower of Baba Saheb Ambedkar. Later, I learnt that he had actually worked with Baba Saheb as a research assistant. Bhagwan Das had compiled and published Ambedkar's writings and I had quoted at length, in my book *The Demystification of Law for Women* (1986), Ambedkar's letter of resignation in protest against Nehru's refusal to pass the Hindu Code Bill which would have made radical reforms in Hindu law. I was shocked that Nehru had misrepresented Baba Saheb, saying he resigned because of illness. Bhagwan Das had also given me another book, which I had not read carefully enough to understand its full political import. The book was *The Untouchables: Who Were They and Why They Became Untouchables*, published in 1948. In this book, Ambedkar addresses the question of vegetarianism in India. He links it to the banning of beef eating. I quote an important passage:

> That the object of the Brahmins in giving up beef-eating was to snatch away from the Buddhist Bhikshus the supremacy they had acquired is evidenced by the adoption of vegetarianism by Brahmins. Why did the Brahmins become vegetarian? The answer is that without becoming vegetarian the Brahmins could not have recovered the ground they had lost to their rival, namely Buddhism. In this connection it must be remembered that there was one aspect in which Brahminism suffered in public esteem as compared to Buddhism. That was the practice of animal sacrifice which was the essence of Brahminism and to which Buddhism was deadly opposed. That in an agricultural population there should be respect for Buddhism and revulsion against Brahminism which involved slaughter of animals including cows and bullocks is only natural. What could the Brahmins do to recover the lost ground? To go one better than the Buddhist Bhikshus not only to give up meat-eating but to become vegetarians—which they did. That this was the object of the Brahmins in becoming vegetarians can be proved in various ways…

When Soe wanted to get married to Thin Thin Aung in 1998 he wanted to have a Buddhist wedding. I contacted Bhagwan Das and asked whether he could help the Burmese couple. Bhagwan

Das arranged for the marriage in the Dalit temple in R.K. Puram, Delhi. It was the last time I met Bhagwan Das.

~

Baba Saheb's writings and insight into the origins of Indian vegetarianism have become even more relevant today with the Hindutva forces trying to convert Muslims and Dalits and tribal people into vegetarians. In May 2017, during the month of Ramzan, the RSS held iftar parties in which Muslims broke their fasts with cow's milk and vegetarian dishes. Dalits, too, are being forced to convert back to Hinduism in what is called 'ghar wapasi' or a movement to return home. But this form of Hinduism comes inextricably linked to Brahmanized vegetarianism.

This attempt to impose vegetarianism leads to the question: should Dalits opt to become vegetarian, would they then be accepted as the equals of Brahmins?

In 2011, Sebastian and I travelled right across the Northeast, covering 15,000 kilometres in four months. It was on that journey I discovered that in the eleventh and twelfth centuries Brahmins had gone all over and converted many tribal communities to Hinduism. But none of these communities, even if they were the rulers of ancient kingdoms such as Manipur and Cooch Behar, were accepted even as Kshatriyas, and today they are included in the list of backward castes.[20]

I also discovered that many of the region's insurgencies are rooted in the protest against the imposition of the caste system on tribal communities, and forcible conversions to Hinduism, as in Manipur, where the ancient script was suppressed and the Bengali script imposed, bans on beef and pork were promulgated, and a caste system superimposed on local social constructs.

Sebastian remembers that as a child he was not allowed

to enter Meitei Hindu homes because he was a tribal. Meitei women would not serve him respectfully in the traditional way but would drop the food into his hands because his touch could pollute them.

The heart of India's problems, the stumbling block to her progress and the flowering of her creativity, is the pernicious caste system and until it is annihilated we can never call ourselves a truly civilized people.

~

I was brought up to believe that Kashmir was a paradise where Hindus and Muslims shared a culture of Kashmiriyat. I used to think that the one thing both Hindu and Muslim Kashmiris shared was their love of kahwa. I remember during the Delhi winters, my Dadi made a special tea for herself. It had the fragrance of almonds and cinnamon. She sipped the tea from her metal glass which was so hot that she held it with her sari pallav. It was her version of Kashmiri kahwa. Dadi would give me some of this tea and I loved to slurp it from a saucer.

There was a lovely copper Kashmiri samovar in our house. We never made tea in it, but Amma had explained how it was used and it fascinated me. I have it now. It was only recently that I discovered that my copper samovar is probably a Muslim samovar; Kashmiri Hindus usually have samovars made from brass.

I also did not know that not only are there Hindu samovars and Muslim samovars, but tea is also divided along religious lines. Kahwa is mostly associated with Kashmiri Pandits, while the Kashmiri Muslim starts his day with pink-coloured salty tea, which Kashmiri Muslims call noon chai and Kashmiri Pandits call sheer chai.

A Kashmiri Pandit writing in a local newspaper observed:

> However, unfortunately, in Kashmir the Pundits cannot share their deep feelings with Muslims. For Muslims 90% of Kashmiriat consists of only Islam which is the overpowering force everywhere...in every bond. The remaining 10% is not made up of sophisticated things like music and literature and movies—but more trivial things like kangri, pheran, samovar, wazwaan, Kashmiri vegetables like haakh and nadroo. Even in these day-to-day trivial items of use there is a distinction between Pundits and Muslims. The pheran used by Pundits has a wide border below the knees. The samovar of Muslims is made of copper whereas the 'batta' (Hindu) samovar is usually made of brass. The Hindus do not prepare 'gushtaba' and 'rista' in their weddings although these two are the prime items in a wazwaan (special Kashmiri feast). Kashmiri Muslims have 'harissa' for breakfast in cold winter mornings—whereas many Pundits have not even heard what it is. 'Harissa' is a sort of mutton halwa prepared by boiling the meat overnight.[21]

The prejudices, ignorance and arrogance of the upper caste Hindu liberal is best illustrated by my experience at a tea party I attended. In June 2017, I received an invite via SMS to attend a meeting of a 'select group of women from India on how to reach out to Kashmiri women—the worst victims of conflict...' The meeting was to be held in one of the flats in a south Delhi colony where I live. The meeting began with a friend, Basheer from Kashmir, speaking about the deteriorating situation in the Valley. He made a passionate appeal to the group of women from Delhi to go and meet ordinary Kashmiri women and show them compassion and empathy. His audience comprised women working in the NGO and corporate world. There were several men belonging to the armed forces and wives of officers in the Army and the Air Force.

What shocked me was that no one wanted to listen; they only wanted to tell. One of the army officers gave a brief lecture on the history of Kashmir and said the present conflict was rooted in the Partition of India. He ended his history lesson by saying that Kashmiris alone did not face discrimination; he was often called 'Madrasi' by his Punjabi boss and North Indians made fun of the way Madrasis ate sambhar with their hands.

It would have been no use telling him that even if the conflict was rooted in the Partition and the British policy of divide and rule, it was definitely compounded by the human-rights violations committed by the Indian armed forces; and by the fact that these violations were not acknowledged and the perpetrators were not punished. And yes, North Indians were often both ignorant and prejudiced against South Indians, but they did not as a result refuse to rent their homes to South Indians or suspect every Tamilian of being a member of the LTTE. Delhi did not send in the army to intimidate and humiliate the 'Madrasis'.

There was a young woman dressed in a chic black-and-white kurta who said she was working with Kashmiri women and what the young women really wanted was to become fashion designers. She was working with an army sponsored programme and had trained forty women in fashion designing; Walmart and other multinational companies were helping with the marketing under their statutory obligation to take up Corporate Social Responsibility.

Then there was a break for a sumptuous spread of tea with cheese sandwiches, samosas, burfi and pineapple pastries. Everyone had a good tuck-in and returned to the meeting feeling 'fed up and fulfilled' as we used to say in college.

One immaculately dressed woman with well-manicured hands suggested that the Kashmiri women could be trained as chefs since Kashmiri food was so good. There were other patronizing suggestions as well.

Towards the end of the meeting, one woman who had been silent till then stood up to speak. She was petite, with thick hair dyed red with henna and kept in place with two clips on either side. She kept aside the plate with a pineapple pastry and told us to listen carefully to what she had to say. She quoted Gandhiji about allowing the winds from all cultures to blow about the house as freely as possible. She explained that till a few years ago the children in Delhi ate only butter chicken and black dal but now they were used to having Mediterranean food and fare from all over the world. It has opened their minds. The same could be done for the Kashmiris.

Perhaps she meant it as an analogy. But she did not elaborate. She picked up her plate and finished her pineapple pastry, satisfied she had made a profound intervention.

I could feel some of the angst Basheer and his friends must have felt. It was as if he and his audience were inhabiting two different planets. The world in which Basheer was living and the world in which the audience was living were as different as pineapple pastry and goshtaba. I do not know what could possibly bridge the abyss.

~

Somehow, the incidents at the Kashmir meeting reminded me of the sumptuous dinner I had with our Naga friends Patricia and David Kire in Dimapur on the night of 6 December 1992.

It was a lovely dinner with the usual pork, fish and, what was special, they also offered mithun meat. After the meal I remarked: 'I loved the food; but I wish Nagas served a dessert after their meal.'

We all laughed and then settled down in front of the television to listen to the nine o'clock news. Patricia was knitting, David and Sebastian were sitting comfortably partly watching the TV and partly enjoying the kids playing in front of us. It was an idyllic family scene.

David worked in the State Bank of India and Patricia's father was an Irishman who had helped construct the famous bridge over the River Kwai. Then he had fallen in love with a Tangkhul Naga and settled among his wife's community. I felt quite at home sitting with all of them till my attention turned to the news.

There was a scene of Hindutva kar sevaks on top of the dome of the Babri Masjid in Ayodhya, tearing the mosque down…it had all already happened by the afternoon but none of us knew. The event had had no impact on the Nagas.

I watched the scene in horror. Ayodhya is a few kilometres away from Faizabad, the capital of Awadh—the heart of the celebrated composite Ganga–Jamuni culture of an India of the past, or at least an India of the imagination. Some of Amma's family lived in Faizabad. I watched the images of the mob attacking the mosque with axes, hammers and grappling hooks. Later I learned that the entire mosque had been levelled within just a few hours.

I felt my heart was being torn apart; tears of pain and anger welled up, but I had to suppress them. There was no way Patricia, David or Sebastian could have shared my pain. We lived in the same nation state, but our belonging was defined by totally different histories, cultures and identities.

I knew that the India I had always dreamt about had been destroyed. There would soon be riots and violence…

Patricia's cousin, Nancy, was standing in front of me smiling shyly. She had made rosgullas from rice powder to satisfy my sweet tooth. I forced myself to smile and thank her.

Patricia and David Kire were no strangers to communal

violence. The violence in their larger community could be vicious, ugly and deadly. Sometimes it took the form of conflict between the Semas and the other tribes living in Dimapur; and sometimes it took the form of violence against Bangladeshi migrants. What made the violence so dangerous was that both sides were backed by well-armed and trained insurgents.

~

Where is the hope? I am asked this question often. I believe that the vast majority of our people are not hate-filled fanatics. They are capable of tolerance and love; and my belief is based on the real-life experiences I have had.

In the late 1980s I was in Meerut. I had been living in Hashimpura, at the home of a man who made scissors whom we called Chachaji. I was there to document the human-rights violations that had taken place in the Muslim-majority locality of Hashimpura following communal riots in the summer of 1987. On the 22nd or 23rd of May that year, the U.P. police had picked up more than forty men from the locality and taken them to Ghaziabad, where they had shot them one by one and dumped their bodies into an irrigation canal, Gang Neher. One of the boys had escaped by pretending to be dead and he had reported the matter to Syed Shahabuddin (1935–2017).

Shahabuddin Sahib, like my father, had been invited to join the Indian Foreign Service by Nehru, and he had distinguished himself. But he had later resigned and devoted his energies to writing about the conditions and problems of Indian Muslims. When he started his monthly journal, *Muslim India*, he had invited my father to be on its board and Papa had accepted.

Shahabuddin Sahib phoned to ask me to go to Meerut and see if I could find out what had happened. I filed a case in the

Supreme Court on behalf of the victims and later continued to work there along with other human-rights activists.

After the horrors of those days, the first wedding was to take place in Hashimpura and I was invited. It was of the daughter of a man we all called Soofiji. His son was one of the men shot dead near Gang Neher. With great love and affection Soofiji told me that he had made special provisions for all his Hindu guests; there would be puris, kachoris and vegetarian dishes.

This was the U.P. tradition and the Kashmiris of U.P. and Delhi also used to have special food for their Muslim guests during their weddings.

I told Soofiji that I would much rather have the food made for his own family and Muslim neighbours and friends. Of course, I much prefer biryani to puris anyway, but on that occasion I wanted particularly to identify myself with the community which had been the main target of the communal violence. Soofiji was pleased by my gesture of solidarity.

Some friends who had helped with the rehabilitation and legal work in Meerut also came for the wedding. I had committed all of them to having the Muslim food, not realizing that Aditi Phadnis was a vegetarian. Soofiji served the food to us himself, and he lovingly put a plate of mutton biryani in front of Aditi as well. I saw Aditi put a piece of meat into her mouth and swallow it before I could tell Soofiji that she was a vegetarian. Later Aditi said she did not want to make distinctions on such an occasion. And she did not want him to know.

I cherish the memories of moments like these, when people crossed all barriers of religion and community to extend solidarity to each other.

Another such moment was when I accompanied a Burmese refugee woman on her quest to find rented accommodation in Delhi.

The woman's name was Zothangsanpuii (Puii) and she was a Chin from Myanmar. She had taken part in the national uprising of 1988 against army rule and when there was a military crackdown, she, like many others, took shelter in India. But instead of a warm welcome she was arrested for illegal entry and locked up in Imphal jail.

I managed to get her out of jail and received permission from the court to take her to Delhi and try and get her the protection of the United Nations High Commission for Refugees (UNHCR). I succeeded in getting her a certificate from the UNHCR (without fully realizing it, I had set a precedent in refugee law), and the UNHCR then helped her to find a rented room.

One of the rooms was on the outskirts of Delhi in a semi-rural area. The house owner was a farmer from Haryana and he had several rooms around a central courtyard. When we arrived, we found the owner's daughter washing a huge pressure cooker at the hand-pump installed in the middle of the courtyard. The pressure cooker belonged to an aged Muslim Afghan refugee who was sitting on his charpai, smiling at us. He was affectionately called Babaji by the local people, almost all of them Hindu, including his landlord's family. The landlord's daughter complained that Babaji did not eat vegetables at all, he only ate beef. He was old and couldn't do all his work himself, so she helped out. When she spoke to us, she was washing the pressure cooker in which he had made beef. Babaji also used a part of his UNHCR stipend to make kheer for the children in that colony.

Puii took to Babaji and they got on famously. She asked him whether she could buy some pork in the market. Babaji looked a little distraught. I thought he was upset and was about to tell Puii that Babaji was a Muslim and did not eat pork, but before I could say anything, the old Afghan said: 'I am so sorry, I do not know where to get pork. But I will take you to the market and we can find out.'

We were sitting in Babaji's small room and I noticed an embroidered picture of the Kaaba. He saw me looking at it and he smiled and told me that his landlord's daughter had made it for him. I left Puii in the safe hands of a Hindu landlord and Muslim refugee. She, a Methodist Christian, already felt at home with her new acquaintances.

~

I am always fascinated by people crowding around street vendors; it is a sight I never tire of. I see girls of all classes and ethnicities pop gol guppas into their wide open mouths; the Sikh taxi driver enjoy his chole bhature; the lady in a sari and with a bindi take home mutton kebabs. And I see workers claim their city confidently, enjoying their pav bhaji. It is in the streets of India, around the stalls of street vendors, that I see hope for the future of Indian democracy.

5

GLOBALIZATION IN GOA

In 1997 I fell ill. Delhi's pollution and stress made my condition worse, so Sebastian and I decided to shift to Goa—lock, stock and books. We sold my DDA flat in Munirka Enclave in Delhi and moved to a small flat on an island called Chorao in the river Mandovi. In order to reach the island, we had to cross the river in a ferry at Ribander.

It was difficult getting used to our new home and we would drive to Miramar beach and eat at one of the shacks. The menu offered a choice of Goan, Indian, Continental or Chinese food. I remember the fluffy cheese omelette, which was exceptional.

One of the waiters was a man called Luis. We discovered he lived right behind our flat in Chorao. Luis lived in a small laterite house, but there were no doors or windows. He spoke fluent English and seemed well educated. One day we did not see him when we went to eat at the shack and learned that he'd had a fight with the owner and was now jobless. After that we would see him wandering around the village, drunk. He did odd jobs for people and then drank up all he earned.

We were settling down into life in a Goan village and every day we learnt something new. A lot of what we learnt about Goan culture and history was from the culinary delights Goa had to offer.

We woke up the first day in Chorao to the incessant sound of a strange horn. We rushed to our balcony to find a man on a cycle surrounded by our neighbours choosing from various kinds of freshly baked bread. We were told that the special aspect of this bread was that it was fermented by using toddy. Most bakers had started using commercial yeast instead, because the price of toddy had been steadily rising. It took us time to learn the names of the different kinds of Goan bread sold by the Poder: crusty, hot and fresh pao, poyi, katre and many other kinds of bread. The word Poder itself is derived from the Portuguese word for baker, Padeiro; a daily reminder of Goa's colonial past.

Most days we were not up early enough to catch the poder. But we were awake and alert by the time the fish-vendor brought fresh fish in a basket tied to the back of his bicycle. Sebastian rushed down and bought lots of fish—depending on the season, we got sardines, mackerels and many others whose names we were yet to learn. There were also women fish sellers, who came with big baskets on their heads; they walked all the way.

We had already acquired a taste for Bebinca on our very first visit to Goa, when we drove down from Delhi to Bangalore via Goa in 1993. Now we indulged ourselves on this lovely dessert.

Bebinca is a layered cake and when I first had it, it reminded me of the thousand-layer cake someone had brought for us from Malaysia. It was only after we started living in Goa that I discovered that Bebinca is named after a nun called Bibiana. According to Odette Mascarenhas, a food critic, the nun created the dessert from the egg yolks that were left over after the white had been used for starching their clothes. Bibian used the leftover egg yolk to make the dessert and people called it 'Bebinca' after her.

We also learnt that Bebinca was a part of the Catholic cuisine;

Hindu Goans had other sweets. There were other differences in their cuisine. The Goan Catholics used vinegar while the Hindus used kokum or tamarind to add a tangy flavour. Our Goan Hindu friends told us in all seriousness that the Catholics' fish curry did not taste good because they put cumin seeds in it.

Later, when we made Goan Muslim friends, one of them told us that although they went to the feasts or weddings of their Catholic friends they did not eat there because the meat was not halal. When I told him that among the Kashmiri Pundits there was a tradition of serving separate food cooked for Muslim guests, he was surprised.

In Chorao we looked forward to our guests from outside the state, but the most difficult part was coping with their food preferences and their reactions to local Goan cuisine. Our guests from Kerala, Husain and Zaida, enjoyed the seafood but maintained that the cuisine in Kerala was so much better. After a day or two with us, Husain insisted that Zaida would cook to prove his point.

Then there was the Bengali couple who also enjoyed Goan fish, but were overjoyed when they accompanied us to buy rahu from Bengali fish vendors.

And then there were my Kashmiri guests from the Valley. They just could not eat the Goan fish. They said it was uncooked because it was not deep-fried!

At one time our neighbour was a Dalit from Andhra Pradesh. He was learning opera singing at the Kala Academy. Being an opera singer, he needed to practice singing so he would go off to the hills around Chorao and sing to his heart's content. He complained bitterly that the Goans did not know how to cook pork. And our Naga friends, too, complained that the Goans chopped up the pork into too small pieces and used too much masala. It never occurred to any of these people that their inability to appreciate Goan cuisine could be a reflection of their own limitations.

But this worked both ways. Ulka, our Goan friend, could not believe that anyone could not like Goan cuisine. She had never eaten anything else and had grown up believing that Goan Hindu food was the best in the world. She was surprised that I hadn't always liked coconut and that all our vegetables were cooked without the benefit of coconut oil, coconut milk or grated coconut. Such a thing was inconceivable!

Ulka said after she met us she realized that there were other kinds of food; and she even watched MasterChef on television and a new world opened up for her. She began to eat pizza, although she never took to it.

In the beginning I found Ulka's attitude parochial but then I realized my ability to eat different foods was also the result of an elite culture which had no real roots anywhere.

~

My health improved day by day; and soon I was able to walk and slowly I began to read and write. I was well enough to take up my first case in Goa towards the end of 1998.

The UNHCR informed me that there were two Iraqi men in Vasco police station; could I see whether they qualified to be refugees under the mandate of the UNHCR?

The two Iraqis turned out to be brothers who had escaped from Iraq on a ship they thought was going to Europe, but it had landed in Vasco, Goa. They had been arrested because they had no travel documents, tried in a court and convicted. After a year in jail they were released, but as they still had no travel documents, they were kept at the police station. Ulka offered to take us there.

The police officer in charge was kind and compassionate and he allowed the elder of the two, Hazeem, to go out so that I could meet him in Panaji instead of having to make a trip all the way to the police station in Vasco. Before deciding on what legal steps could be taken to get the two Iraqis out of detention, I had to know their story.

Hazeem told me their story with his limited vocabulary in English. He said he and his younger brother had the same father but different mothers; and they had many brothers and sisters. Their father had been jailed by Sadaam and he died in custody and the elder brother, too, was executed. Their house was blown up. Hazeem did not know where his other brothers and sisters were, but he and Anwar had fled to Iran in 1991-92 where their aunt lived. They did not like Iran because the women 'talked too much.' Hazeem smiled and had a twinkle in his eye when he said this, knowing I would react to derogatory remarks about women.

I did not disappoint him. I said his reaction to the women in Iran was typically Arab. He did not like Iranian women because they were more assertive and independent-minded than those in Iraq. Hazeem enjoyed provoking me and despite the limitations of language, his humour and humanism shone through even in those trying times.

Hazeem was determined to get to Europe and so the two brothers decided to walk through the desert to reach their destination. In the desert they came across a sheikh who gave them shelter and he killed a sheep in their honour. After they had feasted, Hazeem took out money to pay and the sheikh was very angry. He said: 'You cannot be an Arab if you pay for hospitality.'

The two brothers could not reach Europe and went back to Iran. In April 1997 they went to Bunder Abbas Port, where they found an Indian ship, *M V Ratnadeep*, bound for a place called Vasco de Gama, which they thought was some place in Europe.

I do not remember how long they said it took them to reach Vasco, but they had nothing to eat except vitamin tablets. The younger brother became ill with tuberculosis.

When they landed in Goa, they were put in jail for illegal entry into India. Hazeem said the people were very good because his fellow prisoners, the majority of whom were non-Muslims, told him one day that it was Eid and he should say namaaz. The other prisoners gave him a prayer mat and they celebrated Eid in jail. He got the impression that in India the relations between Hindus and Muslims were nothing but cordial.

I filed a petition before the Goa High Court. I explained that the two brothers had run away from political persecution in their country and had a right to seek the protection of the UNHCR. I wanted the High Court to allow them to go to Delhi and apply for refugee protection. I had used the same arguments many times before in the Gauhati High Court when I got Burmese refugees out of Imphal jail. I attached the Gauhati High Court's orders.

The judges said they could not allow two Iraqis the freedom to move around freely; after all, who knew if they were terrorists or not? But these judges did not put on record their speculations when they summarily dismissed my petition.

There was little to do against this wall of prejudice. I phoned the UNHCR and had a very long conversation, trying to persuade them to issue a certificate to the two brothers; at least a temporary certificate so they could travel to Delhi. It took all my skills as an advocate for them to agree; and finally the two brothers were free.

Sebastian and I took the two brothers to a restaurant in Panjim. At the end of the meal, when they brought a finger bowl, I saw that Hazeem was about to drink the water. This reminded me of a story Papa had told me to illustrate British diplomacy.

Queen Victoria was once at a diplomatic reception in London. The guest of honour was the maharaja of one of India's princely states (in other versions of the story, he is an African chieftain) All went well during the meal until, at the end, finger bowls were served. The guest of honour had never seen a British finger bowl, and no one had thought to brief him beforehand about its purpose. So he took the bowl in his two hands, lifted it to his mouth, and drank its contents down. For a moment there was silence among the British guests and then they began to whisper to one another. All that stopped, however, when Queen Victoria silently took her finger bowl in her two hands, lifted it, and drank its contents! A moment later, five hundred British ladies and gentlemen simultaneously drank the contents of their respective finger bowls.

I would have liked to share the story with Hazeem, who had a rare sense of humour; but he did not know enough English. But I saved him the embarrassment by quickly showing him what the bowl was for.

In the night we had a celebration. Hazeem and Anwar offered to cook biryani, the Iraqi way. Our Goan friends, Sabina and Subhas, offered their kitchen in Panjim. All the while the brothers were cooking, Sabina was in and out of the kitchen looking to see how they cooked. She gave us a running commentary; she found it unbelievable that they did not use masalas. Goan food relies heavily on masalas.

Hazeem and Anwar stayed with us in Chorao for several days. One day, when Sebastian and I came back home after visiting a friend, we found they had made gallons of grape sherbet and filled every bottle they could find. And they had spent all their money—they had eighty rupees when they came out of jail. It was rather like the story in the film *Babette's Feast*.

The next day, I booked their flight tickets for Delhi. When Sebastian tried to offer money, Hazeem refused to take it. I sat down with the two brothers that evening and said they were now a part of our family, they were like sons to us, so I had the right to give them money.

Hazeem finally accepted the money, saying, 'You can be Anwar's mother, but I am too old to be your son.'

I met them again when I went to Delhi for my father's funeral. I asked them to come for the memorial meeting. I reminded them they were a part of my family. They arrived that day carrying a massive thali with a rich dessert; it was more than enough for our immediate family members.

I found out that Hazeem had borrowed money from an Ethiopian refugee to buy the ingredients for the dessert. When I asked him why he did not bring the Ethiopian friend, he said because the man made his money from trafficking in drugs. It was not good to bring such a man into the family.

I am sure Papa's spirit was pleased with the presence of the Iraqi guests at his funeral.

After a long struggle I helped the two brothers finally get resettlement in Denmark. Hazeem phoned after some time to say that he was unhappy there because the locals did not like people with black hair.

Before leaving, Anwar had given me a gift. He told me that if I wanted to test whether the honey I had bought was pure or not I should dip a dry matchstick into it and strike the match. If the honey were pure, it would light easily. Fake honey of sugar-fed bees does not light easily. Anwar said he had learnt this from their father who was a sweet-maker in Iraq.

~

The drive from Panaji to Ribander is down the 3.2-kilometre-long causeway often referred to as the longest bridge in the world. It was built by the Portuguese in 1633–34. The official name of the bridge is Ponte Conde de Linhares and legend has it that the Jesuits built it in a single night under the light of a single lamp.

It is a lovely drive—the sea on the left and the saltpans on the right visible through the bushes and mangroves. We saw neat piles of salt made by the traditional salt-makers and we learnt that the Goans bought this salt for an entire year. A few months after we moved to Chorao, we read that the government had banned traditional salt making. The ban was imposed as per the guidelines issued by the International Council for the Control of Iodine Deficiency Disorder, courtesy the WHO and UNICEF.

There was a public outcry against the ban. Goans were appalled that the traditional salt-makers, the Mittkaars, and the salt-pans, Mittache Agor, which have been around for 1,500 years, were to be wiped out of the landscape. The protesting NGOs and opposition parties accused the government of banning the traditional salt at the behest of the multinationals who, they alleged, wanted monopoly over the salt market.

The opposition exposed the false basis of the state government's sample survey regarding iodine deficiency in Goa. The survey showed deficiency among 49 percent and goitre among 35 percent of the population. It meant every second Goan lacked iodine in his or her body while every third person was suffering with goitre—which was obviously not the case. The figures exposed the absurdity of the survey.

At the time, I had no idea that the ban in Goa was in pursuance of a national-level ban on sale of non-iodized salt for human consumption issued many years earlier; Goa was among the last states to enforce the ban.

The ban in Goa came four years after the agitation led by the Kutch Small-Scale Salt Manufacturers Association to stop Kandla Port from handing over 15,000 acres of land to Cargill, who had submitted a proposal to build a US $15-million salt manufacturing unit. On 31 August 1993, they organized a march called Ulta Dandi March from Dandi to Ahmedabad. This march reversed the route that Gandhi had taken in 1930.

On 2 October the struggle was to enter a decisive stage, with an indefinite blockade of Kandla Port, when Cargill abandoned their project. They said they had arrived at their decision because of purely commercial reasons, not the agitation.

Finally, in September 2000, the Government of India lifted the ban after facing opposition from all corners of the country. But the condition of the salt workers remains pitiable.

~

I saw for myself the wretched conditions of the salt workers when we went to the Little Raan of Kutch in February 2011. Sebastian and I were driving from Goa to Delhi when we turned off to see the Little Raan. We stayed at a rustic resort and were taken for a safari to the saltpans—they are a stunning sight. It seemed as if we were driving through a glistening white field with a lake ahead of us. The lake was a mirage.

There were other tourists with us; some of them came to observe the rich wildlife, mainly wild asses; others were interested in the birds. Suddenly, the vast silence of the Rann was broken by the sounds of music and song. There, in the middle of the desert, a Telugu film was being shot!

In the scorching heat, we came across a small family of salt-makers. We stopped to talk to them. They live in the desert from October to June, dependent on the government water supply; school, hospital or any other amenities are far, far away. This was just one small family of the thousands of salt workers living well below the poverty level.

~

Salt has been a major issue in the Northeast region of India. In Vijaynagar, Arunachal Pradesh, salt is sold for Rs 150 a kilo. At the same time, on the other side of the state, near the LoC, the local chamber of commerce, the association of gaonburas (influential village chiefs) and various NGOs have submitted memorandums to the Arunachal Pradesh government as well as the Centre for resumption of people-to-people trade with Tibet. They favour an arrangement where the 'governments and armies of India and China have no role to play'. This is because for centuries the Arunachal villagers used to trade with Tibet, taking rice, chillies and animal hides in exchange for rock salt.

~

Salt was, of course, an important source of revenue for the colonial rulers. The famous Dandi March led by Gandhiji was against the salt tax imposed by the British. It wasn't only a political movement, it was a movement literally for life; we do not always remember how harsh the salt tax was for the vast majority of people, who could no longer afford to buy salt.

During British rule there were terrible famines resulting in the death of millions of people. This was in part because the British exported most of the food grain, facilitated by the new railway lines. But official reports also show that many of the deaths were not due to plain starvation, but due to lack of salt. One study of sixty-two villages showed that only 12 percent of deaths were ascribed to 'hunger' alsone, while on the other hand, 63 percent were due to 'fever and bowel complaints'. As we know, salt depletion is often fatal in those illnesses. Even during the famines, the British gave no remission of the salt tax.[22]

In November 2009, while driving from Delhi to Goa we stopped at Navsari and went to see the beach at Dandi. I tried to imagine Gandhiji and the Congress workers, but all I could see was a dirty beach, the sand almost black with pollution.

In Delhi there is massive, glistening black sculpture depicting Gandhi's iconic Dandi March of 1930 in the heart of the city, easily visible on Sardar Patel Marg, near Willingdon Crescent. It has become a landmark in the city, though it is not known as the Dandi March sculpture or the Salt March or anything that could remind us of the great event in our freedom struggle. Instead, taxiwalas and autowalas refer to this grand sculpture as the 'Gyarah Murti' or the eleven statues.

~

Is that all that the Dandi March means for the Government of independent India? A commemoration without substance or meaning? Why was the Government of independent India following in the footsteps of the colonial powers and helping big corporations to reap profits from salt and allowing the people to starve?

I had plenty of time to ponder on all these questions as we got used to life in our island village in Goa, slowly getting into the rhythm.

~

The moment we awoke in our flat in Chorao, we waited to hear the honking of the fisherman on his cycle with a basket of fish tied to the back and covered with a blue tarp. Our help, Nanda, would call out to the fish vendor in her musical Konkani and go downstairs to buy something for us. She would choose the freshest mackerels or sardines or whatever the season brought. At that time the price of the mackerels was one rupee each, and Nanda managed to get us one extra because we bought for Rs 10 to Rs 20, depending on whether we were alone or expecting guests.

Nanda would stuff the mackerels with lots of masala and then pan-fry them on a griddle. The Hindus did not have their fish without a coating of rava or semolina; although in the past rice powder was used which to me tastes much better. Once we found a menu offering 'naked fish'! That was fish without a coating of rava or rice powder.

The fisherman on the cycle did not bring shrimps or prawns. Those were sold by the woman who came walking slowly with a wicker basket full of shrimps, clams or shellfish.

If we wanted to have kingfish or red snapper, Sebastian would go to the jetty in Panaji and buy fish from there. It was at the jetty we saw diplomats coming with their iceboxes to pack large quantities of lobsters, prawns and other seafood. We also saw large trucks fitted with cold-storage facilities which bought seafood for the five-star hotels.

From my balcony, I watched our neighbours buying fish. They would walk up to the fisherman from whom Nanda was choosing mackerels or sardines for us. I felt deeply embarrassed that our neighbours, with families much bigger than ours, bought much less fish than we did and sometimes none at all.

The immediate neighbour on the left was a Hindu family and the son was a carpenter. They lived in a small house without a water connection. Their source of water was the water-pump on the road; I had seen long lines of people waiting for the water, which came twice a day, though sometimes the pump was dry for a week or more.

The neighbours on our right were a Catholic family. There were, in fact, three families living in a small concrete house in a large compound. The house had been built with money sent by the younger son who had worked in the Middle East, but who had died leaving a widow whose name was Cynthia.

Cynthia told me she had started working in a shrimp factory and I would see her return late, looking very tired. She had to walk because there was no bus service at that hour. She felt bitter: her husband who had worked in the Gulf had sent money to his parents to build the house, but after he and his parents had died, there was no one to support her and she had to work in the factory.

I wondered what her working conditions were in the factory but I dared not ask in case she felt embarrassed. I had had occasion to listen to the working conditions of women employed in the fish industry when the National Fishworkers' Forum organized a public hearing on the matter and had invited me to be a judge along with Justice V.R. Krishna Iyer, Justice Janaki Amma and Supreme Court advocate Indira Jaisingh, in Ernakulam on 23 June 1995. That was the first time I heard testimonies of women working in the fish industry.

The women said they lived in crowded rooms, often thirty to thirty-five in a room, with just one or two bathrooms or toilets,

At the public hearing organized by the National Fishworkers' Forum.

and no privacy. They were often not allowed to have even a day off or any holiday. They suffered from numb, blistered fingers, back and leg pain, and were subjected to unhygienic conditions.

We found that most of these women were used as forced labour and were in servitude. Cynthia must have faced similar problems, because I noticed she had stopped going to the factory after a few months.

~

While we enjoyed the fresh seafish we also longed for river fish which tasted better in the curries we usually made, such as fish with fermented bamboo shoot or a Bengali fish curry with mustard sauce. That is how we discovered that Mr Ganguly, a retired Bengali gentleman, sold river fish including rahu, katla and occasionally pabda on Sundays in a corner under the Mandovi bridge. He said this was a 'social service' he was doing.

Later, we discovered five Bengali brothers who sold fish at their home in Banastarim, a village famous for its weekly markets. Now they even have a shop in Porvorim and sell Bengali vegetables such as patol (parwal in Hindi). The brothers would phone to tell us when they had hilsa and we would rush to buy our favourite fish. It has too many fine bones for most of our Goan friends, so we were not able to share the joys of eating hilsa with them.

It was because we bought rahu that we found the Bengali and Bihari community of Goa. Each community made its own arrangements for its own cuisine.

~

In the monsoons there was a ban on fishing. I remembered how I was always taught that we should not eat fish in those months which don't have the letter 'r', so in the months of May, June, July and August no fish was usually eaten in my parents' home. But the Goans who found it difficult to do without their fish relied on dried fish or fish para, which is a pickled fish.

The importance of fish in Goa was encapsulated by the state's poet laureate, Bakibab Borkar, in one of his poems:

Please Sir, Mr God of Death, Don't
make it my turn today, Not today,
There is fish curry for dinner.

As the years passed by, we noticed that the prices of fish in Goa were going up. And we began to hear about the shortage of fish as well. In 2010, Baban Ingole, one of Goa's leading marine scientists, said that Goa was sitting on the brink of a fish famine. That year, Goan fishermen netted 23,831 tonnes of mackerel, but three years later, in 2013, the haul had shrunk to virtually half at 12,994 tonnes. Sharks, which find their way to tables in Goan homes and restaurants as 'ambot-tikh', a red, spicy-sour preparation, have all but disappeared, their haul reducing sharply from 3,159 tonnes in 2010 to 281 tonnes in 2013. The harvest of prawns too had depleted from 9,970 tonnes in 2010 to 8,380 tonnes in 2013.[23]

It was not only climate change and pollution; the tourism industry was also responsible for the growing shortage of fish in Goa. Ever since we moved to Goa, we have seen the huge refrigerated lorries loading fish and seafood and carrying them for export and to the five-star hotels to satisfy the growing number of tourists, both domestic and international.

~

Sebastian and I would go to a small restaurant owned by a fisherman. It was at the far end of the Miramar beach and the whole family lived there. Only the fisherman spoke a little English; the rest of his family spoke Konkani and Portuguse because they had lived in Mozambique, another of Portugual's colonies.

One day I watched the fisherman spread his net and I was still there when he pulled it in. I had decided to wait there while Sebastian attended to some work. It was quite soothing and I enjoyed watching the fisherman. But when he had pulled the net out I noticed that there was very little fish. He looked crestfallen. It was a tiny glimpse into the crisis facing traditional fishermen all over the country.

Then one day, we found the fisherman and his family had disappeared. We were told they had been evicted for violating the law which forbids any construction within the High Tide Line. But hotels continued to privatize beaches and violate the same law that was used to evict the poor struggling fisherman.

Environmental activists have been active in Goa. There have been protests against construction near the sea which is destroying the ecology of the coast. The development on the coast has already displaced the traditional fishermen and toddy-tappers. Now luxury tourism is keeping Goans from enjoying the beaches which have become the de facto private property of five-star hotels. Armed security guards keep away ordinary people.

The activists also stopped the building of golf courses, which diverted all the water resources from the villages to the gardens and resorts. It was the activists in Goa who had first exposed the ugly and destructive face of the tourism industry.

~

Traditional fishermen are at the receiving end of the global trade, environmental problems and the tourism industry. I remember interviewing fishermen in Kerala in 1999. One of them was

K.C. Alosius, who told me that when he used to go fishing as a child he could not imagine that there could ever be a shortage of fish; the sea seemed to be limitless. Infinite. But now he knew from his own meagre catch how the trawlers had wreaked havoc by not allowing time for breeding and by polluting the seas.

I knew a little of the conditions of the fishermen because of my association with Father Thomas Kocherry (1940–2014), the priest who had spent his entire life organizing fishermen, first in Kerala and then all over India. I met him, along with union leaders from twelve states, in Bangalore. I was deeply impressed that he had devised a method in which they had a system of whisper translations, so all of them understood the proceedings of a meeting or even when they talked to individuals, like me.

In March 1999 when I was teaching law in Cochin University, Tom Kocherry invited me to the office of the National Fishworkers' Forum in Trivandrum. He wanted me to meet two fishermen: Peter, aged 48, and Lawrence, aged 51, who had recently been imprisoned. The two men were out on parole and Tom said I should listen to their story.

Peter and Lawrence, two fishermen from Puthra village in Kerala, had been convicted of murder and given life imprisonment. They told me that before the fishermen had been organized or a union formed, the church leaders had amassed great wealth by exploiting them. Every family had to give a subscription of Rs 100 and the parish priest collected tax (they called it tithe) on the sale of coconuts and the fish catch.

Then came Father Tom Kocherry and two other priests along with the Medical Mission sisters and they stopped all this illegal extortion. They insisted on the election of the parish priest, so people had control over their parish. They also organized a crèche for the children and started a library. In addition, they raised money for the parish by selling coconuts collected from the trees growing in the church compound.

The rich people were upset and they started making money by distilling liquor and selling it to the poor. They also owned the ration shops where the fishermen had to go to buy basic necessities like sugar and kerosene.

By this time, Tom and the other priests had organized the union, and the Kerala Independent Fishworkers' Federation was registered. They fought for their rights around a whole range of issues.

One of the union activists was Nicolas, who was caught by the rich men, tied to a coconut tree and beaten to death. They tried to make it look like a suicide, but the fishermen knew that Nicolas had been murdered by the goondas of Gilbert, a rich man.

In 1991, Gilbert became even more powerful because he had the backing of the Congress Party, which had come to power. He and his son, Eugene, terrorized the fishermen and raped the women; sixty families were thrown out of their village and had to stay away for six months.

The fishermen were so angry that they beat Gilbert's son to death. In that murder twenty-one people were convicted, including Peter and Lawrence. But, according to Peter and Lawrence, the trial was unfair. They said the conviction was based on the evidence of a witness who claimed that he saw the murder but was, on his own testimony, one and half kilometres away.

Peter and Lawrence said that when they were coming out on parole, the other convicted fishermen told them to murder the members of Gilbert's family—Gilbert himself had died of sickness. I asked the fishermen whether they had felt like taking that advice. They stood looking so dignified before me, and they smiled sadly and replied: 'We don't feel like taking revenge.'

~

Tom Kocherry led a nationwide campaign to stop the Indian Government from opening the country's fishing industry to the growing fleet of 2,600 large foreign trawlers. Commercial fishing has not only destroyed the livelihood of millions of fishermen, but its impact has also been disastrous in many other ways; the most dramatic has been the depletion of fish in the oceans.

I had asked Tom whether he could arrange for me to meet the other fishermen so that I could record their stories. He organized an interpreter and sent me to various villages to meet the fishermen. One of them was Jacob from Kannamaly village in Kerala. I am reproducing Jacob's story from my notes:

> The first time I went to sea was when I was thirteen years old. I have five brothers and three sisters and I was the youngest. We were in a bad financial situation because my father was ill, so I had to leave school.
>
> Normally the first time we go to the sea we go with our father or elder brother, but since father was not well I went with fifteen elders of the village, but not relatives. I was the only child.
>
> I learnt swimming in the village pond which was on the way to school; but there are many fishermen who do not know how to swim. The only qualification needed was that we should be able to keep floating with only our head above water.
>
> The first time I went to sea I felt very tired. And I felt sea-sick. Everyone feels this and the sensation can last two or three weeks. That is why for children, although they are very enthusiastic to go to sea, the first time is very frightening.
>
> The first job for the child is to get into the sea and hold one end of the fishing net and then the rest would be laid out. We measure the length by holding it from the chest to an outstretched arm; so a net would be 80 full chest lengths, or around 100 metres. The boat goes right around and comes

back to the spot where the child is. Nowadays, the net is much larger and children are no longer used.

In those days, we went in small boats which often overturned, especially near the shore where the waves are greater. That is why we could not carry much and we would have to drink the salt water. That is why we were not healthy.

Before putting the net out, they study the colour of the sea and read the clouds and wind direction. I do not know these things.

Now they have motorized boats and kerosene is expensive. We need Rs 6,000 for diesel per day (about 300 litres). The boat is also expensive and it can cost up to Rs 15 lakhs, so several of the fishermen pool together and buy one boat.

Many fishermen have to leave their traditional profession and go and work on big trawlers.

~

I did not meet Tom after 1999. I learnt of his death through the media. It was then I realized that he had taught me so much about the fishermen but had said so little about his own role. I met Tom Kocherry's companion, Father James. He too was extremely humble and spoke very little. He did, however, offer some ginger wine he had made himself. In honour of the priests who led the epic struggle for fishermen, I give Father James' recipe:

GINGER WINE

Ingredients

- 10 litres of water boiled and cooled
- 2 kgs of ginger
- 3 oranges (skin of one and juice of all three)
- 50 grams of yeast
- 1 kilo of small bananas

Method

- Mix all the above ingredients, strain and keep in bottles for some time.
- Pour in caramel for colour.

I have not tried to make the wine but I tasted the one Father James had made. It was delicious. Here's a toast to Tom and his comrades.

~

Goa cuisine does not consist only of fish curry and rice. While the Goan Catholics also love their fish curry and rice, they also have their chorizo or sausages, and bread. The Goan sausage is small and when dried looks like red beads strung in rows. It is mixed with spices and is bursting with flavour.

I read a story in the local newspaper about Antonia Da Silva, a sausage maker who has been selling sausages all his life, like his father and grandfather before him. Every day he chops 90 kilos of meat, seasons it with salt and garlic, marinates it with 10 litres of his own homemade palm vinegar, and adds the other spices to make five thousand sausages a day. In addition, he sends four thousand sausages three times a month to Mumbai and fifteen hundred to Swindon in the UK, where there is a substantial community of Goans.

And this is the story of just one sausage maker! I wonder how many sausages are made every day in Goa?

There are many things you can do with the sausage. The most common is sausage in pao or pav, the local bread. The Goans also make scrambled eggs mixed with sausage, and a sausage pulao which is absolutely delicious. Sebastian and I have found that adding even one or two beads to vegetables such as brinjals, ladies' fingers or just the good old potato can give the dish a delicious flavour. Sebastian even makes sausage-stuffed paratha. It is such a wonderful example of fusion food.

In a sense Goan cuisine, like so many others, is a testimony to the wonders of fusion cuisine. Perhaps the best example is the feijoado, a stew made by cooking rajma beans with pork and beef along with spices.

I was surprised when I saw this dish on the menu in Brazil where it is considered the national dish. Some people say that the dish was invented by slaves from Angola who worked in plantations in Brazil. The slaves made the dish from the leftovers that they got from the dining tables of their masters. Feijoado is also commonly prepared in Portugal, Macau, Angola, Cape Verde and Mozambique.

~

The first time I became aware of Goa's strong connection to Africa was when we used to buy our sausages from the village famous for making them, Aggassim. A man who looked African could be seen stuffing the red mixture of sausage meat, spices and vinegar into the intestines. We learnt that he was a part of the Siddi community of people who had been brought to Goa as slaves by the Portuguese.

We would be reminded of Goa's connection with Africa from time to time. For instance, when we first tasted chicken cafreal we were told that it was a spicier version of the dish from Mozambique. It was introduced into Goan cuisine by the Portuguese and the African soldiers serving under the Portuguese. The preparation includes green chillies, fresh coriander leaves, onion, garlic, ginger, cinnamon, pepper, chilli, mace, clove powder and lime juice or vinegar.

There was a flourishing market for African slaves in the sixteenth and seventeenth centuries and Goa was one of the most important ports connecting Mozambique, Mauritius, Macau and Ceylon (Sri Lanka). The human cargo was handled by Goan traders such as the Mhamai Kamat brothers.

The 350-year-old Mhamai Kamat house near the old Secretariat is a major landmark in Panaji. The Mhamai Kamats consist of ten families, which are spread out but congregate here for the Ganesh Chaturthi festival. The house is thrown open every year around the time of this festival when more than a thousand guests are given a traditional feast with sixteen vegetables.

The traditional cuisines are slowly giving way to different types of new food. With a shortage of land and the adverse effects of climate change governments are already preparing for a time when many things we eat and take for granted would have disappeared.

Our friend Dr Francis Ngachan, who headed the Indian Council for Agricultural Research (ICAR) in the Northeast told us that Indian scientists had been deeply engaged in conversations with their counterparts to find new sources of food because climate change would destroy the many sources of nutrition on which we depend. As a part of preparations for these changes they had started emu farms in the Northeast. When he first told us this, I had thought it was an outrageous idea.

The emu is the second-largest living bird by height, after its cousin the ostrich. It is endemic to Australia. The emus cannot walk backwards with ease and that is why it is Australia's national emblem as a symbol of the country moving forward. It was unthinkable to me that the emu could become a part of Indian cuisine.

Ngachen says the size of an emu egg is 15 times bigger than that of a typical hen's egg, and is emerald in colour. Each egg weighs 500 to 750 grams. The Australian aboriginals cook emu eggs in an earth oven, in ashes. It is the same way Nagas cook many meats and vegetables. But high-end Australian chefs use emu eggs in desserts such as an emu egg crème brûlée and milk chocolate mousse made with emu eggs.

Ngachen said emu meat and eggs were much healthier than other meats and eggs. Emu meat is lean, low in cholesterol, and high in iron and vitamin C.

I could not believe that by 2017 emu meat and emu eggs had become available in Manipur for consumption; Rs 500 per kilo for the meat and Rs 200 per kg for the eggs. The emus had successfully been bred at the emu farm Salai Agri Consortium Pvt Ltd.

Emu farms are now spread across the country, from Manipur to Karnataka, Tamil Nadu, Kerala, Andhra Pradesh, Maharashtra and Delhi. An emu starts laying eggs once it is three years old and lays 30 to 35 eggs in a year. But rearing emus is an expensive affair and can cost up to Rs 3,000 per emu every month.

People all over the country have started successfully experimenting with emu meat. In Telangana, I hear, people are now buying haleem made from emu meat during Ramzan. In Goa some people have set up a company supplying biologically appropriate raw food (B.A.R.F) for dogs. Their advertisement reads: 'Our complete and balanced emu diet for dogs is made with meat sourced from a responsible and ethical farmer based in Karnataka. We do not add any hormones and it is antibiotic-free. Since emu is "exotic" meat that is fed raw, it has a low chance of causing or aggravating existing allergies. Emu is an easily digestible raw novel protein.'

Here is a recipe from Kerala in case you find yourself buying emu meat sometime soon:

KERALA STYLE EMU MEAT MASALA

Ingredients

- 1 kg Emu meat
- 2 tsp ginger garlic Paste
- 4 tsp red chilli powder
- ½ tsp turmeric powder
- ½ tsp coriander powder
- ½ tsp pepper powder
- ½ tsp garam masala powder
- 8 nos. green chillies (chopped)
- 4 cups water
- 4 tsp coriander leaves
- 6 tsp ginger (chopped)
- 6 tsp garlic (chopped)
- ¼ cup coconut oil
- Curry leaves
- Salt

Method

Step 1 : Cook for 10 minutes

- Add ginger garlic paste, red chilly powder, turmeric powder and coriander powder to coconut oil (2 tsp) and saute for 3 minutes. Add Emu meat, curry leaves, salt and water. Cook this on a low flame for 10 minutes.

Step 2: Fry for another 5 Minutes

- Take a pan, add the chopped green chillies, chopped ginger garlic and coriander leaves and fry them in coconut oil. Then add the Emu meat and fry for 5 minutes. Add the pepper powder and garam masala powder and mix well.

(*Source:* https://chefandbutcher.in/2014/07/07/how-to-make-kerala-style-emu-meat-masala-step-by-step/)

I have not tried emu meat yet; and I do not like fusion food or the new fads in food. I know that globalization will eventually change our diet and our cuisine, but for the time being Sebastian and I are happy to stick to tradition. And in Chorao that was easy because we could not get anything but the local traditional food.

~

Sebastian and I had settled down to our life in Chorao. I was always surprised at how we had been welcomed and made to feel at home, even though he was a Naga from Manipur and I a 'downstairs Kashmiri' from Delhi.

On one occasion when Sebastian and I were flying from Mumbai to Bangkok by Air India, one of the flight attendants turned out to be from Goa. When he learnt we were living in Chorao he had a special request: he was retiring and could I persuade his wife to live in Chorao? He said his wife was also on the aircraft; they were going for a holiday. Of late they had been having differences of opinion on where they should settle after his retirement. He wanted to settle in his ancestral home in Chorao but his wife was not convinced. He brought his wife and seated her next to me.

The wife grumbled and said her husband did not realize how difficult it was to maintain old houses; she complained that he did not understand the practical aspects of living in an ancestral home. I had to agree with her because we ourselves had decided not to buy one of the many old homes that are always for sale in Goa—they are usually damp and attract termites which would be dangerous for my books.

While we were conversing, the flight attendant told us that there were two other flight attendants on the plane who were also from Goa; and unbelievably, all were from Chorao! So there were six of us from Chorao meeting at 36,000 feet in the air.

When we landed, the flight attendant presented us with an expensive bottle of champagne to celebrate. We decided it would be appropriate to share the bottle with our friends back in Goa. So we called our friends and Sebastian managed to pop the cork and poured the sparkling wine into glasses that we clinked together as we had seen people do in the movies. But we were very disappointed by the slightly sour taste and could not finish our drinks!

We were surprised that none of our friends had liked the champagne either, but then we had also fallen victim to the stereotypical image of Goans. Except for the elite, the normal Goan may like his or her glass of wine but the wine-drinking custom is not integral to Goan culture. What the average Goan loves is his feni, not foreign wines or champagne.

However, the wine industry is trying to thrust an alien culture upon the Goans in order to promote their products. It is not just wine that is being thrust upon Goans but an entire culture which is unfamiliar to them. According to Arthemio D'Silva, who oversees sales of wines in Goa from the stable of the United Breweries, Goans still have a long way to go before they truly appreciate wine. In an interview to Goa Streets in January 2013, he said: 'It's my personal opinion from the many wine events, parties and celebrations I've been to all these years that many people drink wine as some sort of status symbol without really appreciating its taste.'

~

We have been witness to the way transnational corporations have been working to reach deep into every home in every village in Goa. Coca-Cola and Pepsi have been busy too. On the ferry going back to Charao, we would often encounter a young man. We used to give him a lift and he told us that he was excited because he had got a contract to sell Coca-Cola. The company would provide him the machine to store the cold drinks.

I am sure the man had no idea that a regular 355 ml can of Coke or Pepsi contains about ten teaspoons of sugar, which is like drinking a glass of the syrup of gulab jamuns. The man just wanted a job; he was not concerned with the struggles all over the world to limit the power of the soda giants. These struggles have been documented by Marion Nestle in her book *Soda Politics: Taking on Big Soda (and Winning)*.

The struggles in other parts of India against these soda giants for consuming vast quantities of water have not had much success.

In 1977, the Indian government had banned Coca-Cola. Many of us were happy because we hoped our local drinks, such as coconut water, sherbets and juices would be saved. But seventeen years later, Coca-Cola was back—and with a bang.

On 24 October 1993, it was reported that Coca-Cola made its official return to India in the shadow of the Taj Mahal. A colourful cavalcade of Coca-Cola trucks, vans and uniformed deliverymen paraded through the streets of Agra to great fanfare, signaling to the world's second-most populated country that Coke was back in a big way.

While our friend was excited about getting the Coca-Cola machine, 175 local bottlers in Goa had united under the banner of the Goa Small-Scale Bottlers Association and were demanding that the government scrap the mega Coca-Cola project coming up at the Verna Industrial Estate, with all the privileges, including a twelve-year sales-tax exemption.

Goa's unorganized soft drink industry still holds over 65 percent market share by selling around six million crates annually, but the local bottlers feared that their market would be wiped away.

~

While the products of these transnational corporations were successfully making their way into the daily lives of unsuspecting Goans, their traditional sources of food were under attack. One such traditional source of protein is the frog.

During the monsoons in Goa, the village boys look forward to catching frogs for dinner. Frogs' legs have been eaten for decades in Goa and even today you can get a plate of frogs' legs along with feni if the barman trusts you not to report him to the police. In Goa, frogs' legs are called 'Jumping Chicken'. Sebastian and I were reminded of the nights back in Imphal when the boys would go with their flashlights and buckets to catch the big fat frogs.

Goa has banned the catching of frogs, and every year before the monsoons there are warnings from the Forest Department that anyone caught in the act would be arrested. There is a big difference between local people eating frogs for their own consumption and big corporations involved in the import and export of frogs' legs. Just as there is a difference between commercialized whale hunting by whaling companies and indigenous people hunting whales for their consumption. The scale is totally different. But the stories that appear in the newspapers blame the Goans for the depletion of this amphibian in the state.

I interviewed a farmer in Chorao, Jagan Nath Pai, and asked him what he thought was the cause of the disappearance of frogs. Pai was sixty-five years old and he had worked on his land ever since he was a young man. He had converted his paddy field into a mango orchard and we stood under the shade of a mango tree and discussed the problem.

The farmer said that in addition to his land he had five buffaloes and so he was totally self-sufficient for his food needs except for tea and sugar, which he had to buy. Jagan Nath is different from other farmers because he is a committed natural farmer. He was converted to the idea after reading *One Straw Revolution* by Japanese author Masanobi Fukuoka (1913–2008). He has not used chemical pesticides since 1993.

Pai says the frogs have disappeared because of the pesticides being used by farmers. The insecticides and pesticides have killed all the insects, and so the frogs have no food to eat. Also, many frogs are killed by vehicular traffic because when people come rushing home they don't bother to notice a frog on the road.

I asked whether his children were also interested in carrying on organic farming. He said his son was a lawyer and like today's youth cared nothing for traditions. He would not stand for a pregnant woman in a bus and would tell her to go by taxi.

I felt embarrassed because I had touched a raw nerve. I could see that the sustainable lifestyle of Jagan Nath Pai would have little appeal to people living in a consumer society.

There are reports that frogs are being exported illegally from Goa. In 2011, a wildlife organization published a report called

'Canapés to Extinction: The international trade in frogs' legs and its ecological impact'. This is the first comprehensive study of the frog-leg market ever conducted and reveals an industry that is systematically devastating frog populations throughout the world, severely affecting natural ecosystems.

For example, the French eat an estimated 80 million frogs a year (that's 160 million frogs' legs). France banned commercial frog hunting and farming in the late 1980s. But that did not stop the French from consuming frogs' legs. The French started importing them from Indonesia, which accounts for around 80 percent of all European imports.[24]

These imports to France not only led to the depletion of the ecosystem in Indonesia, but the Indonesians also lost a valuable source of their protein because frogs are a staple food in that country. Frogs also keep fields free of harmful pests; but with the depletion of frogs, farmers have to import expensive insecticides and pesticides.

The real winners of the international frog trade are the corporations that are often involved in both the export of frogs and import of pesticides. And the losers are the poor people who are blamed for the damage to their own environment and are harassed, arrested and even jailed.

There has been no attempt to regulate the consumption of frogs in the Northeast. The reason is that for the most part there is as yet no large-scale export of frogs from the region as far as I know. But frog meat is a favourite in those parts too.

I remember in 2007 I had a unique opportunity to teach the Constitution of India to some senior members of the National Socialist Council of Nagalim (NSCN-IM). They had decided to study the Constitution of India with great reluctance in an effort to further the Indo-Naga peace process which began in 1997.

Sebastian and I had been involved in the process, and so there I was with a group of Naga insurgents who very reluctantly sat down to look at the Constitution of India. It was the closest reading of the Constitution I have ever done. My students included V.S. Atem, the former Commander in Chief of the Naga Army, who was involved in the deadly ambush at Namthilok in 1982. V.S. Atem was later involved in the peace talks, both in devising rules for ceasefire monitoring as well as the peace negotiations.

My students were fairly diligent but the one question they kept asking was, 'If the Government of India promises something and then backs out, what can we do?' They had in mind Sikkim's 'associated state' status which was taken away a year after its annexation. They were also aware that the autonomy promised to Kashmir had been eroded over time (this was before the Government repealed Article 370 altogether). My honest answer was that legally speaking they could do little other than protest. A sovereign power like India could go back on any promises it made.

At one point we took a break because we needed some documents printed out. Sebastian went to the next room to get the documents printed. I had some other documents on my laptop, so I passed it to Atem so that he could read them while we waited. His eyes fell on a folder on my laptop marked 'Frogs'. He asked what it was and I opened it and showed him the research I was doing for a story on frogs. There was a file marked 'frogs' legs' and he asked what that was and I answered that I had collected some recipes for frogs' legs. Now I had the full attention of my students.

A little embarrassed but unable to resist, one of them asked whether I could share the recipe with them. Of course I could, and I read it out slowly so they could take it down. This is the recipe they wrote down in the notebook in which they had been making notes of the provisions of the Indian Constitution:

FROGS' LEGS A LA PARISIENNE

Ingredients

- 16 lg. Frog legs
- Boiling water
- Juice of ½ Lemon
- Salt and pepper
- 2 eggs, well beaten
- Dry bread crumbs
- Fat, for deep frying
- Onion cream Sauce
- 2 tbsp. butter
- 2 tbsp. all-purpose flou
- 1½ c. light cream
- ½ tsp. salt
- 2 tbsp. minced onion
- 1 tbsp. minced parsley

Method

- Blanche frog legs in boiling water with lemon juice and salt and pepper.
- Drain legs and pat dry.
- Dip legs into eggs and roll in bread crumbs. Deep fry at 370°F for 2 to 3 minutes until legs are tender.
- Serve with onion sauce.

The meeting was being held in Delhi, and that evening I invited my Naga students for an Indian meal. I said it would not include frogs' legs but it would be a memorable one. I took them to the iconic Karim's restaurant in the by-lanes of Old Delhi and we all had a jolly meal of kebabs and koftas. They had never tasted the real flavours of India.

~

Around 2010, Sebastian and I shifted from Chorao to Panaji. One of the reasons was that there was not even a pharmacy on the island and we sometimes needed medicines.

We moved into our new flat and we needed to set up our kitchen. I had always dreamt of having a beautiful kitchen with shelves that magically pop out with a light press of a button and storage place for all the little boxes and jars of masalas. I was delighted when I visited the showroom for Italian kitchens in Panaji. I excitedly told Jitender, our carpenter, to come with me to see the wonders of the kitchens on display and help me choose the fittings and fixtures.

He said he was not interested. And he said if I bought that ready-made modular kitchen, he would charge me a thousand rupees just to fix a screw.

'But why, Jitender?'

And he said: 'It is this imported stuff that is depriving me of my livelihood.'

Jitender came from a family of traditional fishermen who went fishing in the river in Gorakhpur in Uttar Pradesh. But the river had become polluted and there were no fish and the family had become poorer and poorer. Finally Jitender had moved to Goa and in the early months he worked in a furniture shop for Rs 2 a day.

I met him some years after his arrival, about the time he started his own carpentry work. He had done work for me and that is how we had got to know each other. Over the years he had become a real professional and he had brought his younger brothers and taught them the work. He had even bought himself land with a loan that he had paid off; his children were in school and he had bought a small car. Now woodworkers and carpenters are not in demand because people prefer to buy modular kitchens with imported shelves, hinges and fittings. He was about to lose his second livelihood.

I gave up my idea of having a modular kitchen and asked Jitender to do the job—and he did an excellent job. He did allow me to buy a few accessories, though.

~

Living in Panaji meant we could visit the beaches more easily and we often spent the evenings in a shack enjoying our meal as the sun went down into the sea.

Looking at the crowded beaches in Goa today, it is difficult to imagine a time when the beaches were just empty, wild sand dunes without any shacks, restaurants or five-star hotels, which are a part of the coastline today. Then there were no tourists, only the hippies or Freaks, as they liked to call themselves, with their all-night moonlight rave parties, drugs and nude bathing.

Goa's beaches were discovered by the Freaks. One of the first to arrive in Goa in the mid-1960s was Yertward Mazamanian (1924–2010), widely known as 'Eight Finger Eddie', because he was born with only three fingers on his right hand. When he first arrived, he lived in Colva where there were only a few teashops. He welcomed any Hippie who wanted a roof over their heads or food. He later shifted to Anjuna beach where the only eating place was Joe Banana and that was the address at which the hippies received their post.

We were in Goa when Eddie died, well above the age of eighty. Apparently, he did not take drugs. Perhaps that is why he lived so long, because many of that generation of Freaks had died relatively young. They were followed by a new generation, who still had rave parties and found secluded places to dance nude to trance music.

I discovered recently that there is beer named after the legendary hippie. It is called Eight Finger Eddie Beer.

~

Sebastian and I are quite happy trying out cuisines offered by the cafés in Goa owned and run by people from France, Italy, Germany and Britain; and restaurants run by Israelis, Russians, Peruvians, Moroccans, Japanese, and Kachin from Myanmar. I have found places which serve German pumpernickel bread and French croissants and a café, now closed, which had cheese fondue on its menu.

But there was an ugly side to the culinary paradise. We were shocked to learn from waiters working in the restaurants that the owners discouraged Indians (including Goans) from entering their establishments by putting reserved signs on the tables. These waiters confided in us since they were Tangkhuls from Ukhrul district, Sebastian's home in Manipur.

It was an unofficial apartheid and it could turn unpleasant. The waiters were discouraged from serving the Indian guests and instructed to make them uncomfortable so that they would leave.

~

I once heard a young Indian tourist, who I am sure would describe himself as a 'foodie', enter a restaurant in a hotel in Panaji where we were also eating. He said loudly to his friends: 'Let's try Goanese food.' Now the one thing that Goans hate is being called is 'Goanese' and I could see the Goan waiters cringe. I got up and told the tourist so and the waiter whispered 'thank you' as he went with the menu to our young foodie.

According to Wikipedia, foodie is a word of recent origin and describes a person who 'seeks new food experiences as a hobby rather than simply eating out of convenience or hunger'. So, a foodie is distinguished from a gourmet, who is elitist, and more discriminating than a simple glutton! In their book *Foodies: Democracy and Distinction in the Gourmet Foodscape* (2010), Josee Johnstone and Shyon Buamann observe that the 'single greatest weakness within foodie discourse… [is] the lack of critical reflexivity about foodie privileges, especially in relation to the larger global food system.'

In fact, I have found that many of the foodies I know, mostly children of friends, have little idea about food and cannot distinguish between fast food and good cooking.

I read about how two Dutch pranksters tricked self-identified foodies at a food expo in 2014 into mistaking McDonald's fast food for refined gourmet presentations. Here is a commentary by a reporter with a sense of humour:

> In yet another exploration of the powers of the placebo effect and the human propensity to lie, two Dutch pranksters

tricked a bunch of foodies into singing the culinary praises of McDonald's during a food expo in The Netherlands—and yes, there's a video, and yes, it's hilarious.

The premise of the joke is pretty simple. 'Today we'll be visiting the annual food convention in Houten to serve top of the notch recipes from our high-end restaurant to some food experts,' the tricksters tell us. 'The only problem is, we don't actually own a restaurant, so we'll be paying a visit to McDonald's. We'll pick up some snacks there and present them to the food experts at the convention.' Haha, we think to ourselves, good luck pulling that off, pal.

And then we watch as our affable hosts, Cedrique and Sacha of Lifehunters, proceed to chop and quarter a medley of unsavory looking fruits and McDonald's classics. 'This tomato's been here for at least a year,' quips Cedrique. Which, of course, is entirely plausible.

The two jokesters then proceed to serve their lukewarm McDonald's tastings to foodies and critics under the guise that they're made with wholly organic ingredients, and what ensues is a hilarious example of people's inclination to feign knowledge rather than look like a fool.

'It's a bit softer,' says one food enthusiast. 'But also...also a little more moist.'

Oh?

'It's starting to...I feel some warmth releasing in my mouth,' says another. 'There are a lot of different tastes!' Ah yes, the many flavours of a season-less chicken patty. Say no more.

How resplendent, how sumptuous this Originals chicken patty! cries the fool. But oh, not us. We would never.[25]

~

In the years we have been in Goa the food landscape has changed. The international food industry has entered, bringing its bottles, cans and packages of precooked and processed foods. Now food can be bought at the mall and put into the freezer and warmed in the microwave. Slowly, we too fell victim to the food industry: it may begin with a packet of frozen peas or packaged parathas, but once you are lured into the world of instant food it becomes difficult to go back to cooking an old-fashioned hot meal. In the beginning I thought it was wonderful, but now I know it is only a step away from loss of wisdom, from forgetting our own philosophy of food and sustainable living.

It was during the premiership of Rajiv Gandhi, between 1984 and 1989, that fast food or junk food chains were allowed into India. Then, there were widespread protests against their entry, mostly by environmentalists and political activists. But by the time these chains entered Goa there was only a welcome, without any protests. This is what Aldrid da Costa advised his readers on a Goan website:

> Over the last few years other popular fast food chains have also made Goa their home. We bring to you 5 global franchises available in Goa:
>
> **1. McDonald's** The burger joint needs no introduction. The famous golden arches are famous in every country of the world. Bankrolled with a huge marketing budget, it is seen as a cool place to hang out for young millennials.
>
> **2. Kentucky Fried Chicken (KFC)** The colonel's popular crunchy chicken was welcomed by all when it arrived a few years ago in Goa. So far it has 3 stores based in Panjim (in Caculo mall), Margao and Calangute.
>
> **3. Domino's Pizza** The pizza company was one of the first fast food franchises to open up in the state and it has quite a number of outlets sprinkled across Goa, which include Panjim, Porvorim, Margao, Vasco, Calangute and Anjuna.

4. Pizza Hut The popular pizza chain entered Goa, well after Domino's and has far fewer outlets. It currently operates in Calangute and Margao.

5. Subway Could possibly claim to be healthier than the other options. The 'Sub of the day' is serving up delicious sandwiches in Baga, Anjuna, Panjim and now Mall de Goa, in Porvorim.

Competing with Goan favourites?

Most Goan foodies would rejoice in the fact that they now do not have to get on a train and travel to the neighboring states to enjoy some branded fast food, unlike a few years ago. In a tourist place like Goa, tourists will also feel at home if they can take a break from sampling the local fish curry-rice, to refuel with something a little more familiar.[26]

~

Food scares and fads have not reached the proportions that they have in America, but the newspaper supplements are full of information/misinformation (often contradictory) which cause confusion.

There are enough studies to show that junk food is responsible for the growth of obesity in the world. But junk food can enter in all kinds of insidious ways, such as in the form of packaged cupcakes. In Goa, the cupcake has arrived in a big way. There are innumerable events organized around making and eating the cupcake for children. There is no awareness of the recent controversies in the West over cupcakes which led to several schools in the USA banning them because they led to childhood obesity.

I must confess I had no idea how many calories were packed into the little packaged cupcakes I would have for tea. The American news channel CNN's Dr Sanjay Gupta uploaded a story on the controversies around the cupcake:

Cupcake controversy

There's a story circulating about school districts banning cupcakes and other non-nutritious treats from schools, even for birthdays and other events. Cupcakes, lathered with sticky frosting and rainbow sprinkles…mmm…are under fire.

The arguments are easy to state on each side. On one hand, childhood obesity rates are killing America's youth. The rates are starting to approach 20 percent, and our junk food diets are a large part of that equation. Add in that cupcakes have increased tremendously in size. They used to be golf-ball sized. Some are now bigger than softballs. If there are around 25 kids in a classroom, and several holidays, all of a sudden you have lots of calories on lots of days. Those who oppose cupcakes say they are non-nutritious and have no place in the schools.

There are, however, plenty of cupcake defenders springing up all over the country. In Texas, Democratic state Rep Jim Dunnam has been one of the most vocal. He sponsored legislation to allow parents to bring in whatever they want. He became involved after one of the schools in his district banned a father from bringing non-nutritious food to his child's class for a birthday. Dunnam's argument is that cupcakes aren't the problem. Instead, it is lack of activity and overall diet.

No doubt, it is controversial, more so than I would've thought. One school superintendent, who chose not to be named, actually received threatening e-mails after her school district supported the ban. What do you think? Is banning cupcakes going too far? Or, is it a logical way to target the childhood obesity epidemic?[27]

~

In 2008, we got a call from Yaransho, a Tangkhul Naga research scholar at the Jawaharlal Nehru University. He said he had been barred from entering the campus after students living in the hostel room next to his heard him and other Naga students kill a dog. A FIR was filed against him at the local police station and animal-rights activists demanded his expulsion.

Yaransho had phoned us for some help but we were at the time in Goa so we could do little. Many months later, when we went back to Delhi, I asked him what had happened. He told me that in fact he did not eat dog meat; but he took the blame because he did not want the President of Naga Students Union, Delhi, to get a bad name. It was he who had actually killed the dog. Dog meat is an integral part of Naga cuisine.

I remembered this incident when Sebastian and I went recently on a cruise to Antarctica. That was when I read stories about early explorers and how many of them ate their sled dogs to survive. For instance, Roald Amundsen, the first man to reach the South Pole, returned in good condition, actually having put on weight during his trip because he ate his dogs. Amundsen set off with fifty-two dogs and returned with only eleven. No one condemned him or boycotted him for eating his dogs.

The same year, controversy over dog-eating in China took up media space and coverage. It was the year when Beijing was hosting the Olympics. I watched the stunning opening ceremony on television. But what caught my attention was the controversy over dog meat.

The terms of any discussion on food are always set by those who have economic and political power. Zilkia Janer has analyzed the politics of taste in an article in *Seminar* magazine. I reproduce a part of the article where she compares the Western attitude towards dog meat in China and foie gras in France—both delicacies have raised concerns among animal-rights activists. Professor of globalization and food history, Zilkia Janer writes:

To illustrate how culinary judgments are related to geopolitical power, let's take a look at two foods that are controversial in western countries: foie gras and dog meat. Foie gras, the enlarged liver of forcefully overfed ducks and geese, is a delicacy in France. The production of foie gras is deplored by animal-rights activists and its production has been banned in over a dozen countries. Nevertheless, in France foie gras is protected by law as a part of the cultural and gastronomic heritage of the country.

Many foie-gras festivals take place all over the world under the banner of sophisticated gourmet culture, in spite of local production bans. Foie-gras diners might face occasional protests outside of restaurants, but rarely in a violent way. The historical status of France as a colonial power and as the international arbiter of good taste, although waning, still prevents foie-gras eaters from being characterized as primitives that need to be taught how to eat by all means necessary. The foie gras controversy is an internal dispute in the West, conducted in a respectful manner.

In contrast to the foie gras controversy, dog eating is framed in the 'East vs West' and 'primitive vs civilized' discourses. A dog-eating festival is unthinkable and would be illegal in Western countries, and any dog eating happens in a private, unadvertised way. In the West, the population at large, and not only animal-rights activists, see dog eating as a sign of barbarism. Countries like China, where dog meat is one among many other options, have not been able to defend their dog-eating practice as a part of their cultural and gastronomic heritage. China banned dog meat from Olympic restaurant menus in 2008, in deference to Western visitors. China also cancelled a 600-year-old dog eating festival in response to social media protests, and is considering wider bans of dog meat, even though nobody thinks they will be effective.

It would be unthinkable for France to ban foie gras in

tourist restaurants, much less to consider banning it altogether. The difference here is that, unlike France, China does not have enough international political and cultural clout in the current global power configuration to confidently assert its values. China might be rising in the global economy, but the dog-eating ban is one of many ways in which the Chinese are tacitly accepting the supposed superiority of Western culture. In their bid for equality, many peoples have decided to suppress any marks of difference that more powerful peoples have used to denigrate them. A fear of the consequences of being declared a barbarian by the West is enough for many to conform to Western views, whether it makes sense or not. There is no reason to believe that eating dog is worse than eating beef.

To further illustrate how geopolitical power affects the standing of a nation's cuisine, we should note that India does not have the power to shame the West into not eating beef. On the contrary, many Westerners see Hindu beef avoidance as a taboo that has not allowed Indian cuisines to become modern. Jairam Ramesh, speaking at the United Nations in 2009, suggested that stopping beef consumption would stop the single most important cause of carbon emissions.

This environmentalist message is sound, considering that aside from carbon emissions, industrial beef production is responsible for the wasteful and unsustainable use of water, fuel and land resources. However, his comment did not make headlines in the West, where beef-eating is at the centre of many culinary cultures. Instead, it alienated many sectors in India who are beef-eating and who saw his comment as the affirmation of Hindu vegetarian rule. Ramesh's judgment on beef-eating was radical and ineffective in the West, but controversial and conservative in India. The values and meanings associated to any particular cuisine or food are clearly contextual and related to specific power structures.[28]

In Goa, beef is legal and openly available in the market and restaurants, even though the majority of Goans are Hindus. The Goa Meat Traders Association protested against the way gau rakshaks or cow vigilante groups had started impeding the beef trade.

According to IndiaSpend, a data journalism website, twenty-eight Indians—twenty-four of them Muslims—were killed and 124 injured between 2010 and 2018 in cow-related violence. Almost all of the sixty-three attacks since 2010 involving cow-related violence were recorded after the Bharatiya Janata Party led by Narendra Modi came to power in 2014.

In Goa, the chief minister, with a strong RSS background, had to ensure the supply of beef to hotels and restaurants, otherwise tourism would be affected. So the beef supply has been resumed. But the beef controversy has not been put to rest.

In June 2017, Goa hosted the sixth All India Hindu Convention on the theme, 'Need for Unity of Hindu Community and Saints for Establishing the Hindu Nation'. The convention demanded that the cow be declared a national animal. Around 150 Hindu outfits met in Goa to draw up a programme to establish a 'Hindu Rashtra' in India by 2023; the local BJP, RSS and VHP units distanced themselves from this event. The conclave was organized by the Hindu Janajagruti Samiti (HJS), the sister outfit of Sanatan Sanstha, some of whose activists were accused of the murder of rationalist Dr Narendra Dabholkar in August 2013.

~

Academics, especially historians, have been attacked for pointing out that in ancient India beef was eaten by all, including Brahmins. Many of them have been dismissed as communists or anti-nationals. However, it is impossible to put such a label on India's most respected food historian. The most authoritative books on the history of food have been written by Kollegal Thammu Achaya (1923–2002). As one admirer of Achaya, Marryam Reshii, wrote:

> Combing through ancient and medieval literature—the Vedas, Upanishads, Sangam poetry to the hagiography of Mughal emperors—Achaya chronicled the origins and evolution of almost every ingredient found, and dish made in the Indian kitchen. Having a copy of his books can help you win heated arguments about, say, the provenance of sambhar, pulao (it finds a mention in both Yagnavalka Smriti, a 3rd to 5th century AD text, and 3rd century AD Tamil works), or beef-eating in India.[29]

Rana Gomes, executive chef, Royal Orchid Hotels in Bangalore, rues the fact that not too many people remember Achaya's seminal contribution to Indian food history. 'We Indian chefs should celebrate his birthday as "Food Science Day". His work has influenced me to a great extent in understanding the local cuisine of India, using of ingredients and local fresh-grown vegetables and fruits.'

Achaya documents that the Vedas refer to 250 animals of which fifty are deemed fit for sacrifice and, by inference, for eating. He states in his book, *Indian Food: A Historical Companion* (1994): 'The market-place had different stalls for vendors of meat of various animals, gogataka (cattle)... The abattoirs for domestic animals had specific names, like garaghatama (beef)...'

He also records that Charaka, the father of Ayurveda, recommended the flesh of goat, hare, peacock, porcupine, alligator, jackal—depending on the condition of the patient. My thought: Thank goodness K.T. Achaya is dead, otherwise he would be executed as an anti-national by the Hindu extremists.

~

Hindu liberals have protested; but in ways which do not offer any real challenge to the Hindutva forces. Only on one day in June 2017 did the liberals come out on the streets in several towns and cities to protest under a unified tag—'Not in My Name'—to protest against the killing of Muslims and Dalits by mobs of cow vigilantes.

Amita Dhanda, professor of law at NALSAR, had a comment on the protest on her Facebook page: 'My colleague Harathi Vageeshan asked a pertinent question on the Not in My Name campaign. He said the campaign was unwittingly putting out a very self-regarding morality. Instead of unequivocally stating that killing was wrong no matter in whose name, it was falling into the trap of the Solzhenitsyn principle which allows for "evil to enter into the world but not through me".'

Liberals have also protested against the beef ban by saying eating beef is a matter of personal choice, that it is about freedom of expression and lifestyle. They, including a section of the media, have opposed the beef ban largely on the ground that it violates the right of an individual to choose what he or she wants to eat. However, the ban on beef is not merely a question of the violation of individual civil liberties and human rights. The fact that 300 million Dalits and 15 million scheduled tribes collectively have been socially, economically and politically excluded from society for centuries because of what they eat makes the debate on the beef ban something much more than a question of civil liberties and freedom of choice. And the feeling of insecurity of 150 million Muslim citizens facing threats of violence cannot be assuaged by an assertion of solidarity by throwing iftar parties.

Many critics have pointed out that India is blind to its faults and that can be said especially for the upper-caste Hindu liberals. Liberals in India, as in other parts of the world, are showing a remarkable lack of political imagination when it comes to opposing and countering the rise of right-wing politics. The lack of political imagination is reflected in their analysis and their actions.

The question is not only about the exclusion of Dalits, tribals or the religious minorities from the body politic of Indian democracy. The justification for the denial of the right to dignity and equality to Dalits and tribal communities has been provided by Brahminism; and institutionalized by the pernicious caste system.

The point is not only to show solidarity with the Dalits, tribal communities and religious minorities, but also to recognize our own complicity in their exclusion.

~

The controversies over beef, vegetarianism and cow's milk will not be set to rest by voting out the BJP and bringing in another party. That would be just the first step if you believe, as I do, that every one of us deserves a country where we *all* feel we belong *equally*. That can only happen if we can all at least sit together with dignity and a sense of equality and eat at the same table or on the same patch of floor or ground—and not only eat the food that each one of us relishes but also learn to enjoy the sheer diversity of our cultures and cuisines. We could also make fun of each other, and in the process perhaps get rid of our prejudices… But is this a ridiculous dream when a growing number of our fellow citizens have nothing to eat at all?

AFTERWORD

> Children are amalgamators. They add bangers and mash and fish and chips to saag-gosht and parathas… What is normal for the child is to say: all this I am heir to, all this belongs to me. This is the world that nurtures me.
>
> I was the newest kind of explorer because I existed across so many worlds of belonging.
>
> —Ziauddin Sardar, *Desperately Seeking Paradise: Journeys of a Sceptical Muslim*

One of the most meaningful meals I have had was in November 2021, shortly after I had turned in this revised edition of the book to my publisher. At the table were refugees who had been in India for the past seven or more years. I had chanced upon them a few days earlier in South Delhi's Vasant Vihar. They were in small tents pitched outside the entrance to the India office of the United Nations High Commission for Refugees (UNHCR). They had been camping there for more than four years.

The three refugees who were with us that day came from some of the worst conflict zones in the world: Sudan and Iraq. They were men in their thirties, all Muslim. As we sat together and had the meal cooked by one of the Iraqis, they said they were reminded of their home, where they used to eat together with their families. The refugee from Sudan was from Darfur. His five brothers had been killed in the conflict, and he carried bullet marks on his thin body. His mother and two sisters were in a camp back in Sudan. He said he no longer talked to them because after each conversation they all cried.

All three men said they had chosen to come to India because they had thought India was a place where they would be welcomed. The man from Sudan said Hindi films were very popular in his country and people had developed a love for India. The Iraqis said their aunt had advised them to go to India to escape the ISIS because it was a free country.

But they found on arrival that India had stopped giving refugees residential permits, so they had no right to work, and they had no right to open a bank account, so they could not receive money from friends or relatives either. They had all faced extreme hunger and constant police intimidation. When they showed their UNHCR cards declaring them to be recognized refugees, the police said the card has no value.

The UNHCR had not helped them and had literally shut its gates in their faces. They said all they wanted was to have a home, a family and be able to eat together without fear. They called me 'mother'. They said that just the act of cooking a meal and eating at the same table with Sebastian and me made them feel a little bit better; but each one of them had tears in his eyes.

I did not tell them that I was beginning to feel like a refugee in my own country. I did not face the economic insecurities they faced, but I did feel that I did not belong to a nation becoming increasingly intolerant and violent. It was not the country I had grown up in and loved, despite all its flaws. I did not know how many tables I would be banished from, how many fellow country people I could now find to share my table with.

REFERENCES

1. Hank Cardello, *Stuffed: An Insider's Look at Who's (Really) Making America Fat and How the Food Industry Can Fix It*, 2010
2. P.N. Haksar was a lawyer by training. He joined the Indian Foreign Service in 1947 on Nehru's invitation and later was Principal Secretary to Indira Gandhi, the Prime Minister between 1967 and 1973. He has been called the most distinguished public servant of his generation.
3. https://thewire.in/culture/kashmiri-pandit-kashmir-vegetarianism-hinduism
4. Urmila Haksar (née Sapru) was a trained schoolteacher, who taught Political Science in Gwalior, and wrote her autobiography, *The Future That Was* (1973); she is also the author of *Minority Protection and the International Bill of Human Rights* (1974). She was a member of the Committee on the Status of Women in India which brought out the report *Towards Equality* (1974).
5. http://www.searchkashmir.org/2010/12/bichhua-kashmiri-chutney-from-himachal.html
6. K.T. Achaya, *The Historical Dictionary of Indian Food*, 1998 (2002)
7. Pandit Bros. vs Commr. of Income Tax on 24 March, 1954. Equivalent citations: AIR 1955 P H 42, 1954 26 ITR 159 P H
8. http://creative.sulekha.com/goli-or-marble-soda-bottle-of-mangalore_185393_blog
9. https://blogs.economictimes.indiatimes.com/onmyplate/slow-delicious-in-many-tiers/
10. http://indianmuslims.in/in-praise-of-paan/
11. http://lucknowobserver.com/malai-makhan/

12. K.T. Achaya, *Indian Food: A Historical Companion*, 1994
13. Odette Mascarenhas, *The Culinary Heritage of Goa* (2014)
14. Ali told this story to the presenters of the BBC's Hairy Bikers food show.
15. https://lonelyindia.com/2017/04/14/short-storyfolk-tale-why-khasi-people-eat-betelnuttamol-in-meghalaya/
16. See Mohammad Amir Khan with Nandita Haksar, *Framed as a Terrorist*, 2016.
17. https://food.ndtv.com/food-drinks/happy-eid-2017-the-significance-of-preparing-seviyan-kheer-1428494
18. See Nandita Haksar and Sebastian Hongray, *The Judgement that Never Came: Army Rule in the North East*, 2011
19. I have written the story of how Livingstone came to Goa and worked as a waiter and then how he became an owner of a fine dining restaurant in Goa in my book: *The Exodus Is not Over: Migrations from the Ruptured Homelands of Northeast India* (2016)
20. See my book *Across the Chicken Neck: Travels in Northeast India* (2013)
21. Amit Kushari, 'Kashmiri Pundits and Kashmiriyat' in *Greater Kashmir*, May 28, 2011 www.greaterkashmir.com
22. Roy Moxham, *The Great Hedge of India*, 2001, p.142
23. Mayabhushan Nagvenkar, 'Why is the fish disappearing from Goa's plate?' http://www.firstpost.com/india/why-is-the-fish-disappearing-from-goas-plate-1431139.html
24. https://www.thelocal.fr/20161012/do-the-french-really-still-eat-frogs-legs
25. https://www.bustle.com/articles/45695-dutch-pranksters- trick-food-critics-into-thinking-mcdonalds-is-fine-dining-and- its-hilarious (If you aren't fluent in Dutch, simply turn on the subtitles.)
26. http://www.itsgoa.com/5-global-fast-food-franchises-available- in-goa/
27. http://edition.cnn.com/HEAL TH/blogs/paging.dr.gupta/2007/02/cupcake-controversy.html

28. Zilkia Jamer, 'Assamese Food and the Politics of Taste', *Seminar*, http://www.india-seminar.com/2012/640/640_zilkia_janer.htm
29. http://marryamhreshii.com/about-marryamhreshii/ remembering-kt-achaya-the-guru-of-indian-food-history/

ACKNOWLEDGEMENTS

In the course of my law practice my clients have brought precious gifts for me—some of the more memorable have been: a hive with larvae, a bottle of red ant chutney, dried fish and fruits. People have shared their food with love and generosity and I have won many friends by appreciating different foods such as dog meat, dried eel, or chutney made with umrok, the hottest chilli in the world.

I remember most the fabulous meal in the first few days after the birth of Bangladesh; in the midst of the war, the family catching a fish from their pond and cooking a delicious curry. I remember the meal shared at the jail gate with the brother of a Kashmiri man who had been sentenced to death.

I remember all of you, too numerous to name: thank you.

I would like to specially thank our friends in Goa: Ulka, Sabina and Subhas for all the wonderful meals, and much more.

Aruna Ghose, my editor, who has made my writing so much more readable. Ravi Singh, who has encouraged me in every way possible and for that I am sincerely grateful.

My father, who instilled in me the need to respect all cuisines; Amma, for her love of street food.

And as always, my husband and companion, with whom every meal together is a celebration of life and our love.